GARY LIBRARY
VERMONT COLLEGE
36 COLLEGE STREET
MONTPELIER VT 05602
WITHDRAWN

QUALITATIVE DATA

QUALITATIVE STUDIES IN PSYCHOLOGY

This series showcases the power and possibility of qualitative work in psychology. Books feature detailed and vivid accounts of qualitative psychology research using a variety of methods, including participant observation and fieldwork, discursive and textual analyses, and critical cultural history. They probe vital issues of theory, implementation, interpretation, representation, and ethics that qualitative workers confront. The series mission is to enlarge and refine the repertoire of qualitative approaches to psychology.

GENERAL EDITORS
Michelle Fine and Jeanne Marecek

Everyday Courage: The Lives and Stories of Urban Teenagers
Niobe Way

Negotiating Consent in Psychotherapy
Patrick O'Neill

Flirting with Danger: Young Women's Reflections on Sexuality and Domination
Lynn M. Phillips

Voted Out: The Psychological Consequences of Anti-Gay Politics
Glenda M. Russell

Inner City Kids: Adolescents Confront Life and Violence in an Urban Community
Alice McIntyre

From Subjects to Subjectivities: A Handbook of Interpretive and Participatory Methods
Edited by Deborah L. Tolman and Mary Brydon-Miller

Growing Up Girl: Psychosocial Explorations of Gender and Class
Valerie Walkerdine, Helen Lucey, and June Melody

Voicing Chicana Feminisms: Young Women Speak Out on Sexuality and Identity
Aída Hurtado

Situating Sadness: Women and Depression in Social Context
Edited by Janet M. Stoppard and Linda M. McMullen

Living Outside Mental Illness: Qualitative Studies of Recovery in Schizophrenia
Larry Davidson

Qualitative Data: An Introduction to Coding and Analysis
Carl F. Auerbach and Louise B. Silverstein

QUALITATIVE DATA

An Introduction to Coding and Analysis

CARL F. AUERBACH AND
LOUISE B. SILVERSTEIN

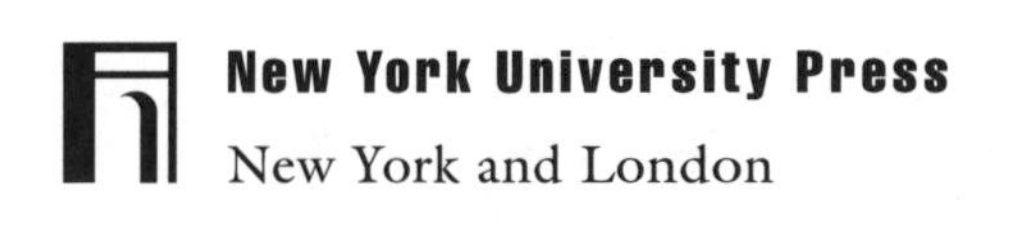
New York University Press
New York and London

NEW YORK UNIVERSITY PRESS
New York and London

www.nyupress.org

Library of Congress Cataloging-in-Publication Data
Auerbach, Carl F.
Qualitative data : an introduction to coding and analysis / Carl F. Auerbach and Louise B. Silverstein.
p. cm. — (Qualitative studies in psychology)
Includes bibliographical references (p.) and index.
ISBN 0-8147-0694-0 (cloth) — ISBN 0-8147-0695-9 (paper)
1. Psychology—Research—Methodology. 2. Qualitative research. I. Silverstein, Louise B. II. Title. III. Series.
BF76.5.A95 2003
150'.7'23—dc21 2003001046

New York University Press books are printed on acid-free paper, and their binding materials are chosen for strength and durability.

Manufactured in the United States of America

10 9 8 7 6 5 4 3 2 1

Contents

■ ■ ■ ■

Preface

The aim of this book is to teach you how to do qualitative research. It will take you through the qualitative research process, beginning with examining the basic philosophy of qualitative research and ending with planning and carrying out a qualitative research study.

This book is part of a movement in the social sciences that is attempting to expand traditional research design and methodology. Traditional research in the social sciences has been characterized by the following principles: formulating hypotheses and testing them statistically, developing scales and questionnaires, attempting to control for extraneous variables by using control groups, and striving to generalize from one sample to an entire population.

Historically, this type of research was accepted as the only correct version of the scientific method. More recently, however, a growing number of social scientists have been reevaluating their approach to empirical research. These researchers have begun to focus on subjective experience, diversity, and historical context. Quantitative research, with its emphasis on operationalizing variables, statistical analysis, and generalizability, is not always well suited to illuminating these concerns. As a result, researchers and theorists are developing alternative, nonquantitative scientific methods, namely qualitative research.

Throughout this book we will illustrate the research process with examples from our own research. We are co-directing a large-scale study of men's development as fathers, the Yeshiva University Fatherhood Project. We will draw our examples from our published papers on Haitian and Promise Keeper fathers. Qualitative research cannot be done without making mistakes, so we will discuss our mistakes, oversights, and failures as well as our successes. You may notice throughout this book that the qualitative researcher is referred to alternately with the pronoun "he" and "she." Some years ago, before feminism changed stylistic conventions, the pronoun "he" would have been used exclusively, falsely implying that the typical researcher was male. In this book we use "she" and "he" in alternate chapters, to indicate that qualitative research, like all research, can be undertaken by both women and men.

The book is organized into five parts. Part I, Getting into Qualitative Research, examines the basic philosophy of qualitative research and contrasts it with traditional quantitative research.

Part II, Planning Your First Research Study, takes you through the procedures for planning a qualitative research study and contrasts them with the corresponding procedures for planning a quantitative research study.

Part III, Analyzing Your First Research Study, deals with the process of analyzing qualitative data, a process called coding. We will describe a six-step procedure that goes from confronting a massive set of verbal transcripts to developing a theory relevant to your research project. This procedure is the core of the book.

Part IV, Designing and Analyzing Your Next Research Study, helps you to take the next step once you have completed your first study. Here we show you how to design and analyze research to further develop your initial study.

Part V, Final Thoughts, is the most personal part of the book. We share with you what qualitative research has meant to us, and the direction our own qualitative research is taking.

Finally, the book has three appendixes. In Appendix A, we explain how to implement our data analysis procedures using NVIVO, a qualitative data analysis program. In appendixes B and C we provide the text of two research articles as models so that you can see how your research can be organized into a publishable article.

Good luck in your study of qualitative research. If you have any thoughts or questions as you are reading the book, please feel free to contact us out our Website: http://members.aol.com/lbsilverst/fathers/

index.html. Just as we want to hear the voices of our research participants, we want to hear your voices. Please let us know which parts of the book have been helpful, and which parts need more explication. We look forward to hearing from you.

Acknowledgments

Writing this book would have been impossible without the assistance of many people. We are grateful to our colleagues at Yeshiva University, Dr. Larry Siegel, Dr. Abraham Givner, and Dr. Irma Hilton for their administrative and personal support of this project in good times and bad. Dr. Barbara Melamed was an early supporter of the Yeshiva Fatherhood Project, as it was moving from idea to reality. We are grateful to Carl's teaching assistants, Dr. Edith Shiro-Gelrud and Mr. Harold Hamilton, for bearing with us while we developed the course material. We received invaluable editorial assistance from Jennifer Hammer at NYU Press, who saw the book through from an initial conversation to the final product, and helped us find the appropriate tone for the book. Dr. Jeanne Marecek and Dr. Michelle Fine paved the way for our making contact with NYU Press, and were the best of readers—equal parts supportive and challenging. Dr. David Klein read our first book proposal and helped us get it into shape.

We cannot mention them all by name, but would also like to thank the students in Carl's course in qualitative research methods, who were guinea pigs for the material in this book. Equally valuable were our research students, who taught us as we were teaching them.

Finally, Louise thanks her husband Barry, who has made it possible for her to engage in the very expensive hobby that is an academic career. And Carl thanks his partner, Sheila, who was always supportive about the writing and other things.

GETTING INTO QUALITATIVE RESEARCH

Part I

1

■ ■ ■ ■ ■ ■ ■ ■ ■

Introducing Qualitative Hypothesis-Generating Research

The Yeshiva University Fatherhood Project

RESEARCH BEGINS WITH CURIOSITY about the world. We assume that you are reading this book because you find a particular phenomenon interesting and want to understand it better. For example, you may have questions about trauma, or fathering, or divorce, or immigration, to list some of the topics that our research team has studied. This book will teach you how to use a very powerful research method, qualitative research, to answer your questions and learn more about your topic.

The field of qualitative research is quite diverse. Some methodologies included in this approach are: participant observation, fieldwork, ethnography, unstructured interviews, life histories, textual analysis, discourse analysis, and critical cultural history, and this list is by no means exhaustive. For our purpose, qualitative research can be defined as follows:

> Qualitative research is research that involves analyzing and interpreting texts and interviews in order to discover meaningful patterns descriptive of a particular phenomenon.

The qualitative approach to research design leads to studies that are quite different from those designed using the more traditional approach. The traditional approach, often referred to as *quantitative research,* leads to *hypothesis-testing* research, whereas the qualitative approach leads to *hypothesis-generating* research. This chapter will describe the difference between the two approaches, and spell out the conditions under which hypothesis-generating research is an appropriate research strategy. We will illustrate the discussion by describing our own research program, the Yeshiva University Fatherhood Project.

Hypothesis-Generating Research as an Alternative to Hypothesis-Testing Research

Perhaps the best way to explain the difference between quantitative hypothesis-testing research and qualitative hypothesis-generating research is to describe how we became qualitative researchers. This occurred as a result of our research program investigating fathers and fathering, the Yeshiva University Fatherhood Project.

We undertook the project for both personal and professional reasons. Beginning with the personal reasons, we ourselves had intense positive and negative feelings toward our own fathers. In addition, we were both actively involved in raising our children, and were struggling to create families where fathers and mothers had an equal role in child rearing.

Our professional reasons stemmed from the fact that traditional theories of child development had neglected the role of the father. They assumed instead that the mother was the most important figure in the child's life, and that the father's role was simply to support the mother. When we began our work, the field had begun to challenge this assumption (e.g., Cath, Gurwitt, & Gunsberg, 1989; Lamb, 1987) and we wanted to contribute to this developing body of research and theory.

We were committed to studying fatherhood from a multicultural diversity perspective. Much of the research on fathering studied only traditional Euro-American families, which we found unnecessarily limiting, both in terms of developing theory and in terms of developing clinically useful knowledge. Thus, we decided to study fathers drawn from the entire spectrum of cultural, ethnic, and sexual orientations. Ultimately, our research included such diverse subcultures as Haitian American fathers,

Promise Keeper fathers, divorced fathers, gay fathers, Latino fathers, young unmarried black fathers, stepfathers, and white middle-class fathers in dual-career couples. To date we have completed data collection on over 400 men.

As we thought about designing research to investigate fatherhood from a multicultural diversity perspective, we realized that traditional quantitative hypothesis-testing research wasn't suitable for our purposes. To explain why, we must describe traditional hypothesis-testing research in a bit more detail. Some of you are already familiar with this material from research design courses, but for those of you who are not, we briefly review it. Hypothesis-testing research may be defined as follows:

> Hypothesis testing research investigates a phenomenon in terms of a relationship between an independent and dependent variable, both of which are measurable numerically. This relationship is called a hypothesis. The aim of the research is to test whether the hypothesized relationship is actually true, using statistical methods.

Here is a simplified example of how a hypothesis-testing researcher might design a study of fatherhood. She would begin by choosing a dependent variable to define the phenomenon of fatherhood, such as a father's affection for his child. To study this variable in research she would have to make it measurable, so she might have the fathers rate their affection for their child on a scale from 1 (the lowest) to 7 (the highest).

Then she would decide on an independent variable, by which is meant a variable likely to have an effect on the dependent variable of affection. She might choose as an independent variable the father's contact with his child, as measured by the number of minutes the father spends in the same room with his child.

Finally, she would state a hypothesis about the relationship between the independent and the dependent variable. She might hypothesize that the more contact a father has with his child, the greater his affection for that child. This hypothesis could be tested experimentally by seeing whether there is a statistically significant correlation between the independent and dependent variables.

This example, although simplified, illustrates the problems we had in using the hypothesis-testing approach to study fatherhood from a multicultural diversity perspective. There were two basic difficulties. First, *we didn't know enough to state meaningful hypotheses, particularly for cultures different from our own.* The hypothesis above is plausible for our own white middle-class culture, but it is less likely to be true in other cultures. For example, a middle-class father may be able to make enough money to support his family with one job. For him, choosing to spend time in his child's presence, rather than in leisure-time pursuits that would exclude his children, may be an accurate reflection of his affection for his child. However, a working-class Latino immigrant father may have to work two full-time jobs to earn enough money to provide tutoring for his children so that they can improve their high school grades. Thus, affection for his children may cause him to spend less, rather than more, time in contact with them.

Moreover, not only did we not know enough to state meaningful hypotheses; *we didn't even know enough to select meaningful independent and dependent variables.* For example, when we studied Haitian American fathers, we discovered that their religious belief was an important variable in understanding how they defined good fathering. We would not have expected this based on our experience with our own secular middle-class culture.

The second problem we had with the hypothesis-testing approach is that *for clinical and theoretical reasons we were interested in understanding the subjective experience of fathers, and because variables must be defined numerically in hypothesis-testing research, they cannot reflect subjective experience.* Even if the study yielded significant results, we would know very little about the fathers' *subjective* experience, that is, what they actually felt about their children. In order to understand something meaningful about his affection for his child, we wanted the following and other questions answered.

What does a father's affection for his child feel like?
What does it mean for a father to be in the presence of his child?
Does he remember times that he was with his own father or mother?
Does he feel nervous being left in charge of an infant, without his wife or another woman present?

In order to address the questions that we were interested in, we searched for a research method that would not require us to state a hypothesis prior to beginning our investigation, and that also would allow us to study subjective experience directly. This led us to do hypothesis-generating research using the *grounded theory* method.

Hypothesis-Generating Research Using the Grounded Theory Method

The grounded theory method allows the researcher to begin a research study without having to test a hypothesis. Instead, it allows her to develop hypotheses by listening to what the research participants say. Because the method involves developing hypotheses after the data are collected, it is called hypothesis-generating research rather than hypothesis-testing research. The grounded theory method uses two basic principles: (1) questioning rather than measuring, and (2) generating hypotheses using theoretical coding.

Questioning Rather Than Measuring

The grounded theory method allows the researcher to acknowledge that she may not know enough to formulate meaningful hypotheses. It uses the research participants as a source of knowledge. After all, they are experts on the phenomenon being studied because they are experiencing it directly. This methodology questions the research participants about their subjective experience and generates hypotheses from their answers. For example, our hypotheses about Haitian fatherhood were developed from what the Haitian fathers said in their interviews with us.

Generating Hypotheses Using Theoretical Coding

The grounded theory method uses a data analysis procedure called *theoretical coding* to develop hypotheses based on what the research participants say. Grounded theory derives its name from the fact that theoretical coding allows you to ground your hypotheses in what your research participants say.

Our discussion so far has covered the application of grounded theory to interview data, and, as you will see later, our illustrative data will be from group interviews, that is, focus groups. You should be aware, however, that the data for qualitative research can also include observed behavior, participant observation, media accounts, cultural artifacts, among others. Thus, the techniques and illustrations we present here cover an important part of the field of qualitative research, but by no means all of it.

With this qualification in mind, qualitative hypothesis-generating research may be defined as follows.

> Qualitative hypothesis-generating research involves collecting interview data from research participants concerning a phenomenon of interest, and then using what they say in order to develop hypotheses. It uses the two principles of (1) questioning rather than measuring and (2) generating hypotheses using theoretical coding.

Describing a systematic method for doing qualitative hypothesis-generating research is the subject of the rest of this book. We will use examples from our own research to illustrate our methodology. We now turn to a broad overview of our research project in order to provide a context within which to understand each example.

The Yeshiva University Fatherhood Project is a large-scale qualitative research study whose researchers have interviewed more than 400 men from many different U.S. subcultures. As we noted previously, these subcultures include Haitian American fathers, Promise Keeper fathers, divorced fathers, gay fathers, Latino fathers, young unmarried black fathers, stepfathers, and white middle-class fathers in dual-career couples.

Each subculture is studied using a sample of approximately 20 fathers who are interviewed in small groups called focus groups, each consisting of 4 to 6 participants. Thus, each study includes 4 or 5 focus groups. The participants are recruited as a convenience sample using a snowball sampling technique. These terms will be defined more precisely later, but basically they mean first interviewing people who are accessible, and then interviewing people known to the original participants. The group interviewer is a graduate student, and is usually but not always a member of the subculture being studied. For example, a Haitian American graduate student interviewed the Haitian American fathers. Three native-born Latinos interviewed 3 of the Latino samples, but the fourth was interviewed by a white Euro-American bilingual school psychologist. One of the gay fathers groups was interviewed by a gay man, but the second group of gay fathers was interviewed by a heterosexual woman.

The focus group interviews are audiotaped or videotaped, the tapes are transcribed, and the transcript is analyzed by a group of four researchers: ourselves, the focus group interviewer, and another graduate student involved with the project. Two consultants from the subculture of the group being studied are also asked to read through the transcripts and comment on them.

After the data are analyzed, a brief synopsis of the findings is brought back to the research participants for discussion. This discussion corrects, broadens, and deepens the researchers' understanding of the participants' subjective experience. The data are then organized by the graduate student and written up as that student's Psy.D. project. At a later date, the findings are reorganized for publication, and a consultant from the subculture is again involved before the final draft of the paper is submitted for publication.

In the chapters that follow, examples from the Haitian American, Promise Keeper, and gay fathers example will be used to illustrate our data analysis procedures. These samples have all been analyzed separately. The articles describing the Haitian American fathers and the Promise Keeper fathers are included as appendixes. The gay fathers have been discussed in a recent publication on gender role strain in U.S. fathers (Silverstein, Auerbach, & Levant, 2002).

PLANNING YOUR FIRST RESEARCH STUDY

Part II

2

Designing Hypothesis-Generating Research

The Haitian Fathers Study

WE WILL NOW CONSIDER how the philosophical differences between hypothesis-generating and hypothesis-testing research translate into research practice. We will contrast a standard hypothesis-testing design with the design of our Haitian Fathers Study. This study was part of our larger research program, the Yeshiva University Fatherhood Project, which we described in chapter 1. The article reporting the results of the Haitian Fathers Study is included as Appendix B (Auerbach, Silverstein, & Zizi, 1997), which you should read at this point.

Hypothesis-Testing Research Design

Research methods courses teach a standard procedure for planning a research study, which goes as follows.

Step 1. Conduct a Literature Review and Identify a Research Problem

Review the research literature to identify an area that we need to learn more about. Pose a small, manageable question about this area. Your research problem is to answer this question.

Step 2. Develop a Research Hypothesis

Propose an answer to your research problem by formulating a hypothesis derived from your review of the literature about how an independent variable influences a dependent variable. This is called your research hypothesis.

Step 3. Operationalize the Variables

Choose numerical scales, tests, or other instruments by which to measure your independent and dependent variables. This is called *operationalizing* the variables. It allows you to test your research hypothesis statistically.

Step 4. Establish a Random Sampling Technique

Decide on the population you want to study and the procedure you will use to obtain a random sample from this population. Your goal is to use a random sampling procedure so that you can generalize your results.

Step 5. Determine Sample Size

Decide on the number of subjects you will include in your research sample. Your goal is to have a large enough sample so that you can get statistically significant results.

These steps are easier said than done, and both novice graduate students and expert researchers struggle with the realities of carrying them out. This approach to social science research is so accepted and standardized that the steps seem written in stone, but in grounded theory, each of the steps takes a different form.

Hypothesis-Generating Research Design Using Grounded Theory

Step 1. Research Problems versus Research Issues

Grounded theory research allows the researcher to admit that he may not know enough to pose a specific question. In fact, he may not know what the right question is until he has finished collecting and analyzing the data. Therefore, instead of reading the literature looking for a specific question or problem, grounded theory instructs him to look for issues that are open and unclear. Research issues are found by looking for perspectives that are left out, and assumptions that need to be challenged.

We designed our Haitian Fathers Study in this way. When we initiated our work, scholars had begun to challenge the assumption of mainstream psychology that the mother was central and the father peripheral to child development (e.g., Cath, Gurwitt, & Gunsberg, 1989; Lamb, 1987). They had begun to acknowledge that the father had an important role in child development. However, much of the early fathering research was "matricentric." Using mothering behaviors as the standard, it tested hypotheses about whether fathers behaved similarly or differently from mothers. Often it was mothers, rather than fathers, who reported on fathering behaviors. Research within the United States relied primarily on white middle-class fathers, ignoring diversity among different subcultures.

Given the limited scope of this body of research, we developed the following two research issues:

1. To study the subjective experiences of fathers, without using mothers as a reference point; and
2. To examine the diversity of fathering experiences among subcultures within the United States.

Step 2. Research Hypotheses versus Research Concerns

Because grounded theory does not assume that the researcher knows enough to formulate specific hypotheses, it moves from research issues to general research concerns.

A basic idea of grounded theory is to choose research participants who have lived through the phenomenon that you want to learn about. Having lived through the phenomenon, they are experts on it. Your research concern is to learn about their lived experience.

In our work, our research concern was simply to learn more about the fathering experience of men from many diverse subcultures. The first subculture we studied was Haitian fathers.

Step 3. Operationalizing Variables versus Narrative Interviewing

The third step in hypothesis-testing research is to operationalize your independent and dependent variables. Doing this is clearly impossible in grounded theory research, because there are no variables to operationalize. What grounded theory research does instead is to construct interviews that allow participants to talk about their lives and experiences.

The procedure we recommend is to ask questions that take the research participants through their history with the phenomenon in question. We call this series of questions a *narrative interview*. The function of reviewing the research literature is to suggest important topics on which the questions should focus. However, when one chooses a research issue about which much is unknown, one cannot assume that current literature can provide an adequate set of questions. The researcher must therefore provide the participants with opportunities to bring up unanticipated topics, so it is important to be flexible about the questions you ask. For example, as we mentioned in chapter 1, the Haitian fathers spoke about the importance of religion in defining the fathering role. We did not anticipate this, but when they brought up the topic of religion we pursued it.

We recommend asking approximately six very general questions. If you ask many more than six questions, the interview will exhaust people, and they will not be able to complete it. If you ask many fewer than six questions, people probably will not give you as much detail as you need in order to understand their subjective experiences.

Getting the questions right is not as important as it might seem. If you ask questions that allow the research participants to talk about what matters to them, what they say will shed light on your research concerns. In most cases, the answers people give are more important than the questions you ask.

For example, in our first two samples of gay fathers, we were still operating under the influence of traditional hypothesis-testing research, and were concerned about "standardization." Therefore, we used exactly the same questions for the gay fathers that we had used for our nongay fathers. It seems almost unbelievable to us now that we did not ask questions specifically about their experiences as gay fathers. Fortunately, the fathers told us a lot about the very different experience of being a gay dad, despite the fact that we did not ask directly.

In the Haitian Fathers Study, we asked the fathers six questions that took them through the development of their fathering experience. We asked

1. When was the first time you thought about becoming a father, and what did you think it would be like?
2. What is your relationship with your father, and how has it affected your fathering?
3. How did you and your wife (partner) go through the process of deciding to have a child?
4. What is being a father like? How did it change your sense of who you are, and what life is about?
5. What are you most proud of, and what do you most regret?
6. How has being a father affected your relationship with your parents and siblings?

Following the questioning, the men were invited to share any thoughts they had not yet voiced.

In our study, we interviewed the men in groups of four or five. We used group rather than individual interviews because group interviews are ideal for exploring collective cultural experiences. Also, people in group interviews resonate to each other's experience, and one person often brings up topics that the entire group then explores. In addition, group interviews are time savers, and allow for sampling a wide range of experiences in a relatively short time. The group interview lasted approximately 1 1/2–2 hours. The group discussion was videotaped and then transcribed. The transcribed interviews formed the text for data analysis.

Step 4. Random Sampling versus Theoretical Sampling

The fourth step in hypothesis-testing research is to choose a population and a random sampling procedure that will allow you to generalize your results. Grounded theory research does not think that random sampling is realistically possible, and approaches generalizability in terms of *developing* hypotheses, not *testing* them.

The Problems with Random Sampling

Grounded theory research is skeptical of random sampling for two reasons. The first is that virtually no hypothesis-testing researchers actually use random sampling. An authentic random sampling procedure would require having a complete list of the population to be studied (a telephone directory with all the Haitian fathers in the United States, for example), and then using a randomization device to select a sample from that list. Except for very large-scale survey research, no one actually achieves this.

Moreover, random sampling is theoretically impossible in studies of cultural diversity. For random sampling to be possible, the researcher would need equal access to all members of a subculture. But members of a subculture are not like beans in an urn, equally likely to be selected by a random sampling process. Rather, a subculture is an elaborate social network that researchers cannot enter at random. They must begin by contacting respected members of the culture and gaining their trust, and build contacts from there. The reality of having to do this rules out random sampling.

Convenience and Snowball Sampling

There are many grounded theory alternatives to random sampling (see chapter 9). The one that we used for our Haitian Fathers Study was a combination of convenience and snowball sampling. Convenience sampling means recruiting whomever you have access to. Snowball sampling means starting with a convenience sample of a few research participants and asking them to select others. These, in turn, are asked to suggest more research participants. In this manner, the research sample grows from the first few research participants, the way a snowball enlarges while rolling down a hill.

Generalizability and Theoretical Sampling

The grounded theory approach to generalizability is sufficiently complex that we will devote a separate chapter to it (see chapter 9). The basic idea, however, is that you must develop your theory before you can know how to generalize it. Once you have developed your theory on a single sample, you can elaborate it further using a procedure called *theoretical sampling*, which entails choosing research participants who have information related to your research concerns. In this way, your *theory*, rather than the requirement of randomness, determines which research participants will constitute your sample. For example, when we analyzed our Haitian father sample we learned that they used religion to construct their definition of fatherhood. We incorporated this into our theory, and chose our next sample, the Promise Keeper fathers, to further explore the role of religion in the construction of fatherhood.

Our Procedure

When we began the Yeshiva Fatherhood Project, very little was known about the experience of fathering among immigrants and people of color in the United States. Deciding which subculture to investigate first was determined by practical considerations. We teach in a graduate school where part of our teaching responsibility is to supervise graduate student research projects. (At Yeshiva, these projects are part of a Psy.D. degree, but they are very similar to Ph.D. dissertations.)

We incorporated students into our research project by having them investigate fathering in subcultures that interested them for personal and/or professional reasons. The first student who did his research with us, Martin Zizi, was a Haitian American father. Naturally enough, he chose to work with Haitian American fathers. This is how our Haitian Fathers Study began.

Step 5. Statistical Significance versus Theoretical Saturation

The fifth step in hypothesis-testing research is to choose a sample size large enough to prove that your research hypothesis is statistically significant. Because grounded theory research is not concerned with testing hypotheses, it approaches sample size differently.

In grounded theory research, in contrast to hypothesis-testing research, sample size cannot be determined in advance. Grounded theory research is concerned with constructing theory, rather than testing it. Each group of research participants interviewed embodies a new opportunity to develop and refine theory. Therefore, in grounded theory research you keep interviewing research participants until you find that new groups of participants are not producing new data that add new concepts to your theory. In effect, you stop increasing your sample when each new group of participants basically tells you the same story that previous groups have told.

Another way of saying this is that you continue interviewing more participants as long as you are learning new information about your research concerns. When you reach the point where you are hearing the same information over again, you have a large enough sample. At this point, new samples will not contribute anything more to your theory. This procedure is called *theoretical saturation.*

Theoretical saturation and theoretical sampling are used together to determine sample size. You use theoretical sampling to select new research participants who are likely to refine your theory. You stop sampling when you have reached theoretical saturation and there is no more to be learned.

In the Yeshiva University Fatherhood Project we chose an initial sample of about 20 research participants, and then did subsequent research in order to develop our theory. We have found through experience that 20 research participants give us enough information for initial theorizing. For our initial sample of Haitian fathers we recruited 20 Haitian American fathers who were members of a Baptist church in Brooklyn, New York to which Martin Zizi, our graduate student, belonged. All of the fathers had been born in Haiti, and had immigrated to the United States during their teenage or early adult years. The majority had been raised in a family with two parents, although some had been raised primarily by their mothers. Their ages ranged from 29 to 60, with a mean age of 40. They had been married from 2 to 34 years, and had from 1 to 5 children. They were predominantly middle class. For a more detailed description of the research sample, consult the research article included at the end of this book.

The Hypothesis-Generating Research Design Recipe

By way of summary, here are the five steps for designing a hypothesis-generating study using grounded theory. The steps parallel the recipe for designing a hypothesis-testing research study.

Step 1. Conduct a Literature Review and Identify Your Research Issues

Review the research literature to locate an area where concepts are open and unclear, where perspectives are left out and assumptions need to be challenged. Your research issue is to explore this area.

Step 2. Define Your Research Concerns

Propose a way of exploring your research issue by investigating the experience of people who know about it from their own lives. Your research concern is investigating their subjective experience.

Step 3. Create a Narrative Interview

Construct approximately six questions that take your research participants through the history of their experience with your research concern.

Step 4. Choose an Original Research Sample Based on Your Research Concerns. Choose Subsequent Samples to Expand and Refine Your Theory

Decide on an initial research sample that is likely to be useful for developing theory about your research concerns. It is often helpful to use convenience and snowball sampling to obtain this sample. Choose your next research samples to further develop the theory you formulated from your initial research sample. This process is called *theoretical sampling*.

Step 5. Decide on Sample Size

Decide on your sample size by continuing to do theoretical sampling until you have reached theoretical saturation, that is, until your research participants fail to provide new data that expand and refine your theory.

3

Qualitative and Quantitative Research as Complementary Strategies

AS YOU ARE DESIGNING AND CONDUCTING a qualitative research study, you may find that it feels very different than the quantitative research studies with which you are familiar. For some researchers this difference is so great that they judge qualitative research to be unscientific. In our view, however, qualitative and quantitative research are complementary, equally valid research strategies. In this chapter, we will describe the differences in order to show the complementary nature of the two approaches. Our discussion will be in terms of six broad themes.

Theme 1. Qualitative Research Directly Investigates Subjective Experience

In the early decades of the twentieth century, subjective experience, because it was by definition not objective, was dismissed as unreliable and therefore irrelevant to "scientific" psychology. The qualitative researcher disagrees with this claim and maintains, instead, that studying subjective experience is an important goal of scientific psychology. Some qualitative researchers focus on conscious experience, some focus on unconscious experience, and some, of course, focus on both. For the methods of this book, the first research question about a phenomenon is: How do people consciously experience it?

In our research on fatherhood, for example, our initial research goal was simply to learn more about men's subjective experience of fatherhood. This goal would have been far too vague and unscientific for a traditional quantitative researcher. As we have seen, she would have been interested in formulating and testing specific hypotheses, for example, that fathers behave differently than mothers, or that divorced fathers behave differently than nondivorced fathers. In order to test these hypotheses, she would have to define variables that can be measured numerically.

From the qualitative perspective these hypotheses would be considered premature. They focused on measurable behaviors before the researchers knew enough about the fathers' subjective experiences to generate meaningful hypotheses and construct variables that captured the fathers' real lived experiences. However, after studying the subjective experiences of fathers to theoretical saturation, it is likely that the qualitative researcher would have generated several relevant hypotheses that could be tested quantitatively. For example, in our study of 20 divorced noncustodial fathers, all of the dads resented the fact that the schools did not send them copies of their children's grades, or notify them of school meetings. An interesting hypothesis to test on a large sample of noncustodial fathers would be: If schools routinely send duplicate notices to noncustodial fathers as well as moms, father involvement with their children post-divorce or separation will increase.

Theme 2. Qualitative Research Incorporates Meaningful Stories in Addition to Measurable Variables

For the traditional quantitative researcher, human phenomena are studied scientifically by converting them into numerically measurable independent and dependent variables. For the qualitative researcher who wants to study subjective experience, restricting data to measurable variables is unnecessarily limiting. The qualitative research paradigm assumes that the best way to learn about people's subjective experience is to ask them about it, and then listen carefully to what they say. People almost always talk about their experience in a storied form. Thus, qualitative research is based on *textual* data rather than *quantitative* data, on stories rather than numbers.

In our research on Haitian fatherhood, for example, the stories our research participants told us about themselves and their own fathers gave us information we could not have obtained by numerical measurements. One such story was that, as children, the men had longed to spend enjoyable time with their own fathers, but had never had that experience because in Haitian culture "adults don't play." Given this history, one of their primary goals was "to be a friend to my child," in other words, to be a relaxed and playful father.

Theme 3. Qualitative Research Allows for Naturalistic Observation and Description, Rather Than Testing General Laws

The ultimate goal of hypothesis-testing research in psychology is to develop generalizable hypotheses, or universal laws, about human behavior. Underlying this goal is the assumption that all people's experience is more or less the same. This assumption may be reasonable in the context of the natural sciences, but in the social sciences diversity and difference are much more likely to be the case than homogeneity and generalizability.

An example of the limitations of this assumption is research on the psychology of women. Most human social groupings generate a complex dominance hierarchy with a resulting diversity of power and therefore of experience. For example, because all human societies are male dominant, at least in our reading of the evidence, one would expect male and female experience to differ significantly. When this has proven to be the case, female experience has often been characterized as deficient (for example, Freud's (1961) theory of the superego or Kohlberg's (1981) theory of moral development in girls).

This tendency to interpret difference as deficit becomes oppressive when the deficit model generates theories that are used to maintain the dominant group's power position. For example, Freudian theory about hysteria in women provided a rationale for excluding women from many public positions because of their "excessive emotionality."

A similar trend exists in terms of diversity among family forms. Poor communities of color within the United States tend to include a large percentage of mother-headed families. This large number of single-mother families is the result of institutionalized racism that has systematically provided inferior educational resources, and therefore job opportunities, to people of color. Because fathering traditionally has been defined as providing economic stability to one's family, large numbers of poorly educated and underemployed African American men have not been able to fulfill the fathering role.

In the 1990s, both popular and scholarly discourse focused on the negative consequences of "fatherlessness" (e.g., Blankenhorn, 1995), rather than on the negative consequences of institutionalized racism which made it impossible for poor men of color to successfully provide for their families. Fatherless families were blamed for many of thc social problems that were actually caused by the poverty and social alienation caused by institutionalized racism. The two-parent married family, a family form more typical of the white middle class, was presented as the solution to these societal problems. This discourse about the importance of marriage provided a rationale for giving preferential access to governmental benefits (e.g., cash bonuses, public housing, job training) to married couples in a way that discriminated against single mothers.

Qualitative research has the potential to avoid interpreting difference as deficit because it assumes that difference, rather than uniformity, of behavior is the norm. The qualitative approach begins with naturalistic observation, that is, detailed description of the phenomenon being studied. Naturalistic observation is useful, not only to identify the lived experiences of the individuals being studied, but also to understand the relevant contexts (social, racial, economic, etc.) of the experiences. From the qualitative perspective, generalizable scientific laws, if they exist at all, can only be developed after taking into account the diversity caused by variations in context.

For example, when we were planning our study of Haitian fathers, we realized that we did not know enough about Haitian culture to state meaningful hypotheses about fathering in that context. If we had generated hypotheses, they would have been based on a middle-class, Euro-American cultural context, rather than on a Caribbean, French-speaking, Afro-Christian, immigrant context. For example, we would not have generated the hypothesis that the men saw their children as "gifts from god," or modeled their fathering behavior on "Jesus as a warm and loving god."

Theme 4. Qualitative Research Is a Tool for Studying Diversity

This theme is a consequence of the previous ones. Qualitative research is particularly well suited to the study of diversity because it does not assume that there is one universal truth to be discovered, but rather focuses on listening to the subjective experience and stories of the people being studied. In our research, for example, we do not assume that there is one universal experience of fatherhood. Instead, we study fathers from a variety of different American subcultures. The Haitian American fathers we studied are one such subculture.

Another subculture is that of gay fathers. Because we were interested in including family diversity in our research, we studied gay fathers as well as fathers in heterosexual marriages. When we listened to their stories, we discovered that they were creating a form of fatherhood quite different from what we could have imagined from our own experience. One distinctive feature was what we came to call *degendered parenting*, in which fathers nurtured and connected with their children in a way usually associated only with mothers (Benson, Silverstein, & Auerbach, 2002; Schacher, Auerbach & Silverstein, 2003).

Our discussion of diversity rather than universality has focused on differences *between* groups, such as the differences between Haitian fathers and gay fathers. But it is important to note that there are differences *within* groups as well. For example, men in a single group of Haitian fathers may be different because of their temperament, position within their family, education, belief systems, and so on. However, our research so far has only focused on between-group differences.

Theme 5. Qualitative Research Uses the Research Participants as Expert Informants

This theme clarifies how qualitative researchers can study diversity without first formulating general hypotheses. It does so by encouraging the researcher to abandon the "expert" stance and treat the research participants as experts on their own lives. It encourages researchers to focus on learning from the people they study. The qualitative researcher acknowledges that people who have direct life experience with a phenomenon know more about it than she does; that *they* rather than *she* are the experts. Instead of having to formulate hypotheses, develop survey instruments, or design experimental procedures that may or may not accurately address the participants' experience, she can ask them directly about their experience, and learn from what they say. In our Haitian Fathers Study, we acknowledged our ignorance about Haitian fatherhood, and were ready to learn about it from the real experts, the fathers themselves.

Theme 6. Qualitative Research Involves Reflexivity; the Explicit Use of the Researcher's Subjectivity and Values

Traditional research assumes that subjectivity and values are sources of bias that can and must be eliminated or controlled. Because qualitative research incorporates these elements, traditional researchers might assume that qualitative research is necessarily biased and therefore unscientific. Qualitative research views the issues differently.

It assumes that subjectivity and values are a necessary part of human interaction and therefore cannot be eliminated or controlled. It requires, instead, that researchers acknowledge their own subjectivity and values, and reflect on them in a systematic and disciplined way. In addition, qualitative researchers believe that their own subjective experience can be a source of knowledge about the phenomenon they are studying. (For a particularly powerful example of this, see Ellis and Bochner's [2000] account of how a researcher's own experience of breast cancer could inform her research on that topic.) Examining the way one's own subjectivity influences one's research is called *reflexivity*, and is a goal of qualitative research.

In our research, we acknowledge who we are, what our values are, and our research agenda. We think that our personal experiences with our own fathers and with our children are relevant to our interest in studying this phenomenon. We believe that knowing about our personal perspective allows other researchers to better evaluate our conclusions.

For example, Louise's father died when she was 5 years old. The loss of her father at an early age generated an interest in knowing about fathers in general. This early loss also stimulated a desire that her husband be very involved with their children, both for the children's sake and also to enable her to be heavily involved in her own career. Carl's experience is as a stepfather who felt as attached to his children as any biological father or mother. Yet he experienced society's bias against stepfathers, that is, the assumption that his commitment to his stepchildren was less than that of a biological parent. Thus, Carl's interest was to learn more about the importance of biology, gender, and attachment in fathering.

We also find that our reactions to what our research participants tell us give us important information about their feelings and experiences. Our experience studying gay fathers who have adopted children illustrates this. When Louise first watched the videotapes of interviews with the couples, she felt upset that the children "didn't have a mother." When Carl first watched them he was astounded at how attentive and nurturing to small children the men in the film were, and could barely believe that what he was seeing was real.

As we reflected on our reactions, we realized that we were caught in the grip of heterosexist bias; in other words, we still believed that children needed a family with a mother and a father in order to thrive. This realization came as a shock to us, because we were under the illusion that we were bias-free! We then began to understand the enormity of the challenge these gay dads were facing: that in order to have children, the gay fathers had to redefine the concept of "family"—for themselves, for their families of origin, and for the broader social community.

ANALYZING YOUR FIRST RESEARCH STUDY

Part III

4

■ ■ ■ ■ ■ ■ ■ ■ ■

Coding 1: The Basic Ideas

NOW THE FUN STARTS! We are going to show you how to develop grounded theory from the interview transcripts, using a procedure called coding. The term coding can be misleading; it suggests a routine mechanical process, whereas developing theory is anything but mechanical. However, because the term coding is firmly established in the grounded theory literature, we will use it as well.

What exactly is a theory? Although volumes have been written on this question, our working definition is straightforward:

> A theory is a description of a pattern that you find in the data.

For example, many of our research participants experienced the fathering role as strained and conflictual. We incorporated this into our theory of how men reconstruct the fathering role, and described it as role strain.

Our coding method is based on the premise that no one is smart enough or intuitive enough to read a series of transcripts and immediately see the patterns within them. In order to overcome this limitation, the coding method is a procedure for organizing the text of the transcripts, and discovering patterns within that organizational structure. By using our coding method you will be able to discover patterns that you cannot see directly in the massive amount of text that you are faced with when you begin to analyze your transcripts. You will then develop your theory from these patterns.

This chapter explains our overview of the coding procedure. The next chapter will teach you the detailed mechanics of coding. We will use the Haitian father interview data to illustrate our coding procedure.

Adrift in a Sea of Data: Your Experience at the Start of Data Analysis

After you finish reading all of your transcripts, you will almost certainly feel overwhelmed by the data, simply because there is so much text to deal with. You will be struggling with two main issues. The first issue is that you are likely to think that *everything* is important. You will be afraid to choose any one thing to focus on, because you will be worried about leaving something out.

Many beginning researchers become stuck at this stage. They are unable to do anything because they assume that there is "one right way" to interpret the data. They are so afraid that they will not be able to find that "one right way" that they cannot begin the coding process. They cut and paste various parts of the transcripts. They call in their research advisers for help with what to do next. In short, they are immobilized.

We have found that the best way to work through this paralysis is to remember that your interpretation of the data will be only *one* of several "right ways" in which the data can be interpreted. We will elaborate on this point in chapter 8, when we discuss the reliability and validity of data analysis in qualitative research.

For now, however, we will simply say that you must be able to support your interpretation with data (i.e., examples of text), so that other researchers can understand your way of analyzing it. If your interpretation is supported by the data, then it is valid, even if there are other ways to interpret the same data. For example, many of the Haitian fathers told us that they had no regrets about becoming a father. This may mean either that the rewards of being a father were so great that they exceeded the negatives, or that the men were denying the negatives. (Or, of course, it could mean both, or something else altogether.) As a theorist you are free to make either interpretation, provided that you can support it with further textual evidence.

Assuring beginning researchers that there is not one right way (i.e., the truth) that they must discover seems to loosen up the paralysis and allow them to begin coding.

The second issue is that beginning researchers, in addition to believing that *everything* is important, simultaneously find it hard to see how *anything* in the interviews bears on their research concerns. This is partly because of the sheer volume of text, but also because the research participants were addressing their *own* concerns, rather than *yours.*

For example, our research concern was to understand the men's subjective experience of being a father. However, when the men responded to our questions, they talked about religion and their church. Our job was to find the connection between their concerns and our concerns. This bridge is often not apparent when we first begin to read the transcripts. We find it helpful to let go of our research concerns somewhat, and focus on what the fathers are telling us. Ultimately, our organizational framework should provide the abstract bridge between our concerns and theirs.

It may happen that the participants have concerns that do not prove to be related to yours. When this happens, it is important to include the participants' concerns even if you do not understand them. If they do not fit into your theoretical framework, those ideas can form the basis of your next research project. If you are truly interested in the subjective experience of the participants, it is their concerns rather than the researchers' that must take center stage.

This is an important point, particularly for researchers doing qualitative research for the first time. Many of our students become quite upset as they begin to analyze their data, because the data do not support the theories that they learned in their training, often theories that we ourselves have taught them. They think that they have done something wrong, and expect us to be angry with them. On the contrary, we think they have done something right, and are delighted. So don't worry if you find your ideas changing as you analyze your data. It's a common occurrence in data analysis, and a sign that the process is going well.

This issue is not just something that happens to beginning researchers.

Figure 4.1

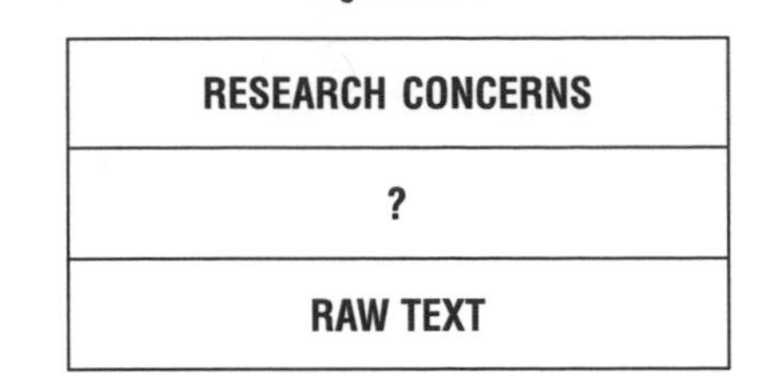

We ourselves have had this experience in our recent work with Latino fathers. We interviewed these fathers to see if we could extend what we had learned about Haitian fathers to other immigrant groups. The questions that we asked the men had to do with their experience of being a father. However, they wanted to talk about something different, namely their experience of being an immigrant. They told us that they were caught between two cultures: They were no longer comfortable with being traditional Latino fathers, but they also didn't want to give up their culture entirely and become Americanized. These participants had to create a hybrid culture, blending elements of each. We came to call this process creolization, and are currently investigating how it comes about.

Although we were ultimately happy with this outcome, initially we were upset about having to rethink our ideas, and embarrassed about not having known any of this in advance. Only later did we realize that having to reformulate our research concerns was not proof that we had failed as researchers, but rather proof that we were succeeding.

In making the point about flexible research concerns, we have jumped somewhat ahead of ourselves, so let us return to what happens as you begin to look at your data for the first time. When you begin any project, you will probably fluctuate between feeling that you must include everything in your data analysis and fearing that nothing really is directly relevant to your research concerns. We characterize this stage as "finding yourself adrift in a sea of data."

Less metaphorically, you will experience a gap between your research concerns and your data, that is, the interview transcripts, as depicted in Figure 4.1. The rectangle at the top of the figure represents your research concerns; the rectangle at the bottom represents your interview transcripts. The question mark in the middle represents the gap between them, in other words, the difficulty in seeing how your interview transcripts bear on your research concerns. Determining how to bridge the gap is the question that we will address in the next several chapters.

When we began to analyze the Haitian fathers' data, we were faced with about 50 pages of interview transcripts, a quantity of text that we considered quite substantial. As we read through the interviews, we felt overwhelmed by the foreignness of what the men were telling us. For example, many of them said that it was necessary to spank children in order to form children's sense of right and wrong, which was foreign to our way of thinking about child rearing. It was as if we had entered a different country, and in a sense we had. Although we were sure that the interview text related to our research concerns, we found it hard to see how.

Swimming to Shore: Small Steps toward Understanding the Data

The central idea of coding is to move from raw text to research concerns in small steps, each step building on the previous one. That way you do not have to immediately see the connection between the raw text and your research concerns; you only have to see as far as your next step. Having taken that step, you will be able to see further and take the step after that one.

You can think of the steps of coding as a staircase, moving you from a lower to a higher (more abstract) level of understanding. The lowest level is the raw text and the highest level is your research concerns.

The steps in grounded theory coding are:

Research Concerns
Theoretical Narrative
Theoretical Constructs
Themes
Repeating Ideas
Relevant Text
Raw Text

We will explain each of these shortly.

When we report our own research, we present the results in an outline form that shows the repeating ideas, themes, and theoretical constructs. Table 4.1 illustrates the one we constructed for the data in the Haitian

Table 4.1

Repeating Ideas, Themes, and Theoretical Constructs for the Haitian Father Study

I. Bicultural Gender Role Strain
- A. Praising aspects of the traditional Haitian father
  1. My dream was to look like my father.
  2. There is no inch of laziness in my father.
  3. I love the way my father treated my mother.
- B. Dissatisfactions with aspects of traditional Haitian fatherhood
  4. My father never said I love you.
  5. Adults do not play.
  6. When they say your father is coming, you run inside.
  7. My father took care of other children and didn't care much for me.

II. Constructing a More Gratifying Definition of Fatherhood
- A. Definition of a good father
  8. My job is to look over the family, being a provider, a protector.
  9. You're not a boss for the children, you're more like a friend.
  10. You have to be there whenever the child needs you.
  11. You call your kid and say I love you.
  12. Jesus was my role model.
- B. An enhanced sense of self
  13. It has changed you; it has reconstructed you.
  14. You're looking at the children growing; it is beautiful.

This is the same as Table B.2 of the Haitian fathers' paper (Appendix B).

Fathers Study. For example, repeating idea number 1 is "My dream was to look like my father." Repeating idea 1, together with repeating ideas 2 and 3, form theme A: *Praising aspects of the traditional Haitian father*. Theme A together with theme B form the theoretical construct I: BICULTURAL ROLE STRAIN. Theoretical constructs I and II allow us to create a theoretical narrative about the subjective experience of the Haitian fathers. (Note that the convention we employ here is to use quotes for repeating ideas, italics for themes, and caps for theoretical constructs. We follow this convention throughout the book.)

Incidentally, the terms we use in this book to describe the steps are different from the language we used in the paper. The Haitian Fathers article (Appendix B) was written in an earlier phase of our project. At that time, we used the term "text-based categories" instead of repeating ideas, and "sensitizing concepts" instead of themes. Our most recent language is, we think, more user friendly.

How the Coding Procedure Works

Relevant Text

The best way to show how the coding procedure works is to take you through the process we used to develop the theoretical construct BICULTURAL ROLE STRAIN. You will see how we developed our theory from raw text, without knowing in advance where the coding procedure would take us.

The first thing we did was to cut the text down to manageable proportions so that we were less overwhelmed by it. We did this by reading through the text with our research concerns in mind. Text that is related to your specific research concerns is called *relevant text*. We kept only the relevant text and discarded the rest, which made the text easier to work with.

For example, one section of relevant text was:

> AG: Sometimes we cannot go to our father and say to our father, "You know something, I love you."
>
> F: Yeah, it is part of our culture. For me especially, even though I never heard such a word from my father's mouth such as "I love you." The way they act to us and the way they deal with us makes me feel that definitely this guy loves me.
>
> L: I tell you my father also never uttered the word "I love you" . . . But you knew he did. I make corrections in my own family. I must repeat to my children, I love them, I do not know, every several hours. Maybe every one hour.

At this point we did not know exactly where we were going with this text. However, we thought that the men's feelings about their own fathers must be related to their feelings about themselves as fathers. Therefore, we thought that this text was potentially important.

Repeating Ideas

Having selected the relevant text, we noticed that different research participants often used the same or similar words and phrases to express the same idea. These ideas are called *repeating ideas*, and they shed light on our research concerns.

For example, in the relevant text above, AG, F, and L all expressed the idea that their own fathers did not express love and affection. They said this in the language summarized as repeating idea number 4 in Table 4.1: " My father never said I love you." We assumed this idea was important because so many of the fathers in the study expressed it.

Other repeating ideas we discovered were:

"Adults do not play."
"When they say your father is coming, you run inside."
"My father took care of other children and didn't care much for me."

These are repeating ideas 4, 5, 6, and 7 in Table 4.1.

In this illustration the repeating ideas occur *within* groups, that is, they are ideas expressed by research participants in the same group interview. However, repeating ideas can also occur *across* groups, that is, they can be expressed by research participants in different group interviews. This is important, because if the ideas were only expressed within the same group, it is possible that the group process influenced people to say things they didn't really mean. The fact that repeating ideas occur across groups argues against this possibility.

Themes

At this point we were beginning to understand the fathers, because we could find groups of repeating ideas that had something in common. We call what they have in common a *theme*. A theme is an implicit topic that organizes a group of repeating ideas. In this case the theme was that the men were dissatisfied with some of the ways that their own fathers had treated them. We later discovered that their fathers were simply behaving according to the traditional Haitian fathering role, so we called the theme *Dissatisfaction with aspects of traditional Haitian fatherhood*.

Another theme we discovered was *Praising aspects of the traditional Haitian father*. Just as there were aspects of the traditional Haitian fathering role that the men did not like, there were also aspects of the role that they admired. In this theme, the men expressed their admiration for their father's strength, responsibility, and hard work. The theme includes repeating ideas 1, 2, and 3 in Table 4.1.

Theoretical Constructs

We were now getting closer to our research concerns. In the same way that we organized the repeating ideas into themes, we organized the themes into larger, more abstract ideas. We refer to the abstract grouping of themes as *theoretical constructs.*

The two themes just mentioned were grouped into the theoretical construct called BICULTURAL GENDER ROLE STRAIN. This theoretical construct expressed the men's conflicting feelings toward different aspects of the traditional Haitian fathering role. The men admired some of what their fathers did, and wanted to emulate them. But they were dissatisfied with other things that their fathers did, and wanted to make changes.

When we began trying to develop theoretical constructs that linked our data to psychological theory, we realized that we needed to know more about Haitian culture. We turned to Haitian social science journals and read about Haitian family structure. We learned that Haitian fathers were very patriarchal, stern disciplinarians who maintained emotional distance from their children. This description contrasted with the progressive cultural construction of nurturing fatherhood in which the father is emotionally close to his children, involved in both caretaking and play. Although the nurturing father role is not yet being enacted by a majority of fathers, it is a mainstay of contemporary cultural ideology about fathering in the United States (LaRossa, 1988).

We then reviewed the data in light of these two theoretical frameworks: the traditional Haitian fathering role and the U.S. nurturing father role. Many of the men told us that they were afraid of their fathers because their fathers used to beat them. They also told us that their fathers had never expressed affection for them, or played with them. This information fit the description of the traditional Haitian father role. The men also told us emphatically that they did not want their children to fear them. They wanted to be a friend to their children, and to be emotionally close to them. These wishes fit the description of the nurturing father role.

However, when these same men were asked directly whether they would use corporal punishment with their own children, they replied that they would, because they believed that spanking was an important form of discipline. We were struck by the incompatibility of these two responses. On the one hand, the men wanted to use a form of discipline that was typical of the traditional Haitian father; on the other hand, they did not want their children to feel the same way about them as they had felt about their own fathers. They wanted their children to be emotionally close to them, a goal characteristic of the U.S. nurturing father.

The inconsistency in their belief system, involving two elements that were mutually contradictory, reminded us of the concept of gender role strain as developed by Pleck (1981, 1995). Pleck pointed out that gender roles are impossible to fulfill successfully because they contain idealized versions of human behavior. For example, attempts to be "masculine" or "feminine" cause individuals psychological strain. There was a similar incompatibility between the Haitian fathers' desire to use corporal punishment as a form of discipline and their desire to not have their children fear them. When we thought about this contradiction it seemed to be driven by cultural differences between Haitian fathering and nurturing U.S. fathering. Thus, we named our theoretical construct BICULTURAL GENDER ROLE STRAIN. An added virtue of this name is that it connected our work with the developing concern with multicultural studies (See Sue & Sue, (2000)).

Theoretical Narrative

Finally, we organized our theoretical constructs into a theoretical narrative, which summarizes what we had learned about our research concerns. The narrative is the culminating step that provides the bridge between the researchers' concerns and the participants' subjective experience. It tells the story of the participants' subjective experience, using their own words as much as possible. However, it also includes the researchers' theoretical framework by including the theoretical constructs and themes in parentheses throughout the narrative. Weaving together subjective experience and abstract concepts brings together the two very different worlds of researcher and participant.

For example, the theoretical construct BICULTURAL GENDER ROLE STRAIN told us that in becoming a father, the Haitian men had to integrate the traditional Haitian fathering role and the modern U.S. fathering role. They had to keep what they liked about their own fathers, and revise the rest. We put this in a theoretical narrative as follows.

> When our Haitian American research participants were thinking about becoming fathers, they had to decide what kind of a father they wanted to be. Naturally, they had their own father in mind in making this decision. Here is the story of how it happened.
>
> The decision about what sort of a father they wanted to be was difficult because they felt conflicted about their own father (BICULTURAL GENDER ROLE STRAIN). On the one hand, there was a lot about him that they admired (*Praising aspects of the traditional Haitian father*). They admired how responsible, hard working, and strong he was; and that "there was no inch of laziness in him." Some of them admired how good a husband he was, and "loved the way he treated their mother." For these reasons, they wanted to be a father like he was; "their dream was to look like their father."
>
> On the other hand, there were aspects of their father that they did not like (*Dissatisfactions with aspects of traditional Haitian fatherhood*). They did not like how emotionally distant he was; how "he never said I love you." Nor did they like his strictness; "when they heard that their father was coming, they ran inside." Also, they were troubled by his sternness; as the saying has it, "adults do not play." Some of them were troubled by the fact that their fathers had children from multiple marriages; "he took care of other children and did not care much for me."

We have come a long way. We began adrift in a sea of data, and ended with a theoretical narrative that bridged the gap between research concerns and raw data. We did it using the text itself, without knowing in advance where we were going. You can do this too, as you will see.

5

■ ■ ■ ■ ■ ■ ■ ■ ■

Coding 2: The Mechanics

Phase 1: Making the Text Manageable

THE NEXT THREE CHAPTERS explain the mechanics of coding—the step-by-step process used to transform the raw text of your transcripts into a theoretical narrative. Our coding procedure has six steps, which are shown in Table 5.1. The six steps are organized into three phases that we have named:

MAKING THE TEXT MANAGEABLE
HEARING WHAT WAS SAID
DEVELOPING THEORY

Each phase deals with a different level of analysis. In the first phase, MAKING THE TEXT MANAGEABLE, you work at the level of the text itself. This is a filtering process, in which you choose which parts of your text you will include in your analysis, and which parts you will discard. In this phase you use your research concerns (Step 1) to select relevant text (Step 2).

In the second phase, HEARING WHAT WAS SAID, you work at the level of the subjective experience of the research participants. The participants may be interviewed in groups, which is our research strategy, or individually, which is the strategy of other investigators. Either way, in this phase

Table 5.1

Six Steps for Constructing a Theoretical Narrative from Text

MAKING THE TEXT MANAGEABLE

1. Explicitly state your research concerns and theoretical framework.
2. Select the relevant text for further analysis. Do this by reading through your raw text with Step 1 in mind, and highlighting relevant text.

HEARING WHAT WAS SAID

3. Record repeating ideas by grouping together related passages of relevant text.
4. Organize themes by grouping repeating ideas into coherent categories.

DEVELOPING THEORY

5. Develop theoretical constructs by grouping themes into more abstract concepts consistent with your theoretical framework.
6. Create a theoretical narrative by retelling the participant's story in terms of the theoretical constructs.

you organize the relevant text into repeating ideas (Step 3) and organize the repeating ideas into more general themes (Step 4).

In the third phase, DEVELOPING THEORY, you work at a more abstract level to group the themes into more general concepts, which we call theoretical constructs (Step 5). Finally, you use the theoretical constructs to create a theoretical narrative (Step 6).

Although we present the steps sequentially, the coding process is not a linear movement from Step 1 to Step 6. Rather, as you code you will find yourself going back and forth between steps. As you become more and more familiar with the data, you will realize, for example, that a repeating idea that you originally coded as reflecting one theme, actually makes more sense grouped with the repeating ideas under a different theme. Or you might decide that two separate themes could be collapsed into a third, more comprehensive theme. Thus, the process of coding is complex and requires patience. We present these steps as a linear progression only for ease of exposition.

In these chapters we will explain how to do the analysis "by hand," that is, by using a word processing program. In Appendix A we will explain how to carry out the same procedures using a qualitative data analysis program. We recommend that you do your first data analysis by hand, so that you can get the feel of the operations involved. Then, later on, you can learn to do the analyses using the computer program.

This chapter will deal with the first phase of data analysis, MAKING THE TEXT MANAGEABLE.

Step 1: Explicitly State Your Research Concern and Theoretical Framework

Your Research Concern

As the first step in looking at the data of a new project, even before you begin actually reading the text, we recommend that you write down your research concern and your theoretical framework on a piece of paper.

> Your research concern is what you want to learn about and why.

Keep this paper in front of you as you begin to read the transcript and think about selecting relevant text.

This exercise may seem superfluous, as you have just finished collecting data, presumably with your research concern in mind. However, we find this exercise to be extremely helpful. Faced with a sea of text, most of us are filled with anxiety. With so much material to choose from, deciding what is important to code and what can be omitted is a daunting task. This is especially true for the beginner, but it also happens to the more experienced qualitative researcher. Therefore, the simple act of explicitly stating your research concern focuses you on what you want to know and why. We have found that this calms anxiety because it becomes a blueprint for making coding decisions.

As you begin to read the text, everything seems important, and it seems impossible to omit anything a participant has said. On the other hand, if you include everything, the amount of data will become unwieldy. With your statement of research concerns in front of you, you can check a portion of text against your statement. Is that particular piece of text relevant to your broad research concerns? If it is, it will be easier for you to decide to include it. If it is not, you will be more likely to feel comfortable about excluding it.

At this point you might find that the text contains something important, but unrelated to your research concern. Remember that research concerns are more inclusive and general than research questions or research hypotheses. Therefore, it is less likely that something your research participants consider important will be unrelated to your research concern than if you were focused on a hypothesis about the specific relations between two variables.

Our research concern, for example, was to learn more about men's fathering experience. This concern grew out of the fact that traditional psychology had focused almost exclusively on the mother-child dyad, and the role of the father in the child's life had been neglected. There was little research on fathers and the father-child relationship. Our research concern, therefore, was quite general.

However, it is always possible that some important information will be unrelated to your research concern, and that you will erroneously exclude it in the early stages of coding your data. For example, we did not realize the importance of religion to the Haitian fathers when we coded the first focus group transcript. However, if an idea is really important, it will be mentioned by more than one participant, and in more than one group. Thus, it is likely to be selected as the coding proceeds. When we realized the pervasiveness of references to religious ideas in the Haitian transcripts, we went back and coded as relevant all of the text that talked about the importance of religion in the men's lives.

Another safeguard against missing important but unexpected data is that each transcript is coded by more than one person. In our project, four people code each transcript. This procedure makes it likely that at least one of the coders will realize the importance of data that the others may have missed. We also use an outside consultant who is a member of the subculture that we are studying. For example, we sent out sample transcripts of our gay fathers focus groups to gay and lesbian psychologists who were experts on gay and lesbian parenting. We asked them to code the transcripts independently, and compared their organization of the data with ours.

Finally, we always present the repeating ideas and relevant text to our participants and ask them if we have gotten their stories right. The ensuing discussions always significantly improve our understanding of the data. Bearing in mind these corrective measures helps decrease our anxiety about the selection process, and encourages us to plunge into the data.

Your Theoretical Framework

In addition to explicitly stating your research concern, you should explicitly state your theoretical framework.

Your theoretical framework is the set of beliefs about psychological and social processes with which you approach your research study.

Your theoretical framework may be organized and detailed. You may be a Marxist, and/or a Freudian, and/or a Piagetian, and/or a feminist. Alternatively, your theoretical framework may be less explicit, for example, humanism. In either case, it is important for you to realize that you do have a theoretical framework that influences what you choose to include and exclude from your analyses. In effect, your theoretical framework determines your biases. Stating it explicitly will force you to acknowledge your lack of "objectivity," and will help you read the text in a more focused way.

Our theoretical framework, for example, is social constructivist and feminist. We believe that gender roles are socially constructed rather than biologically determined. Moreover, our point of view is that the traditional gendered division of labor in parenting roles, that is, father/breadwinner and mother/caregiver, is oppressive to both men and women. Our bias is the belief that both responsibility and power should be shared more equitably. This framework led us to read our text for clues about how men might become more emotionally responsive and responsible fathers.

As you carry out the steps of coding, you will have many thoughts and ideas about what your data mean and what your project is about. We recommend that you keep a record of these ideas, either in a research journal or a computer file, or whatever works for you. These ideas will be important in organizing your data analysis and theorizing.

Step 2: Select the Relevant Text for Further Analysis

As we mentioned, when you start analyzing your text, you will quickly find that you have more than you can possibly use and you need to cut down the mass of raw text to manageable proportions. You do this in Step 2, by selecting relevant text.

Relevant text refers to passages of your transcript that express a distinct idea related to your research concerns.

The method for selecting relevant text is simple and direct. All of your transcripts should be files on your computer. When you encounter a pas-

Table 5.2
Illustrative Heading for Analysis of Relevant Text

Haitian fathers
Focus group 2
Coder: Carl Auerbach

Relevant Text—page 1
January 24, 2003

sage that contains an idea relevant to your research concerns, use the highlighting function in your word processing program to underline the passage. Continue reading until you encounter another passage that contains relevant material, and underline that. Continue in this way until you have worked through all of the transcripts in your study. If you are more comfortable working with hard copies of transcripts, this is an equally valid way of proceeding.

When you are finished, you will have used your research concern to select the relevant wheat from the irrelevant chaff in your transcripts. The underlined passages are the relevant text. Copy only the underlined passages into separate files, one for each focus group (or for each individual, if you are doing individual interviews). Save the files in your larger project folder. Create a separate file for each focus group (or individual interview) transcript.

You will have to keep track of a lot of text and coordinate input from many research collaborators, so maintaining careful and detailed records is very important. Make a header that includes the project, the group, the date you created the file, and the person who did the selection. Qualitative research coding is done by multiple coders, so you will want to be able to distinguish each person's work. If you are keeping memos, record them with the text. For each item of text include the speaker and the transcript page number.

For example, the heading of your relevant text for a particular focus would appear as shown in Table 5.2.

Each coder would create his own files reflecting his selections of relevant text for each of the four focus groups. Similarly, each coder would independently organize the relevant text into a list of repeating ideas.

You may be asking yourself: How do I decide what is relevant? The answer is that there is no rule. Relevance is subjective. Passages are relevant if they seem so to you. Keep in mind the following concerns when you read a passage:

Does it relate to your research concern?
Does it help you understand your participants better? Does it clarify your thinking?
Does it simply seem important, even if you can't say why?

If the text meets any of these criteria, highlight it. These instructions are, admittedly, vague. However, once you try it you will see that you can do it. In fact, as you continue to read the transcripts and become more and more familiar with the data, you will develop a sense of what is important and what is not. (We again point out that our methods focus on what was said. Alternative methods of data analysis focus on how things were said, or what was not said. If you are interested in learning more about these methods, a good place to begin is with the work of Silverman (1993)).

Underlining relevant text can be done in two ways. You can do it quickly and impressionistically, without much conscious thought, trusting that the meaning of what you are doing will be clear at the end. Or you can be more deliberate, writing a memo to yourself in your research journal each time you underline a passage. Use the memo to record why you thought that particular selection was important and any thoughts or ideas stimulated by the text. The method you choose depends on your cognitive style.

In our case, Louise prefers to work quickly, to highlight and see what emerges at the end. Carl, on the other hand, works more slowly. He mulls over each passage, letting his thoughts emerge. Sometimes he reads the transcripts out loud to himself. He usually writes a memo for each selection. Below we illustrate the memo method. However, you can dispense with the memos if they do not work for you.

An example will clarify what is involved in selecting relevant text. Read through the text of Table 5.3, which is a segment of a transcript from the Haitian father data. In the table, the relevant text is underlined and bracketed. The excerpt begins with the moderator's question about becoming a father. Then L responds, then AG, then L again.

Table 5.3

Transcript and Underlined Relevant Text from the Haitian Father Data

Moderator: What was the first time you thought about being a father, and what did you think it would be like? Did you have any models or reference points?

L: Actually [the first time I thought about becoming a father was very early in my life. Probably I, I guess because of my upbringing—as I was brought up in Church and it was always a serious matter to me. I never went out with a girl without thinking that this is the girl I could possibly marry.] Therefore, I always had it in my mind what it would be like. Well, I did not have strong views of what I would be like, what I had was knowing that I would be good toward the people I'd be dealing with. I did not know how I'd be that first time but I knew I would be a loving father. I did not have a picture of how I was going to be but I just knew I was going to be good toward the people . . . So . . .

AG: To me I would say it is very different. When I left my country and I came here in 1983, [I was scared to become a father. As a Christian I was afraid not to meet the proper woman to become my wife in order to become a father. When I met my wife and realized that she was a Christian and looking behind at how my father raised us, I decided to become a father at that time.] [Fortunately, I had my father as an example I would say. He has been with my mother since I was little, and I would say he is still an example for me.]

L: Mine would have been a combination of people. My father would definitely be one of those people because [my father was a very good father. He is a guy who has justice; you cannot make him tremble in front of situations.] He sits, analyzes, and comes to a conclusion. There are several pastors in my life I have come to admire, in the way some of them were. They also play a part, in that it is going to be a combination of people. My father was the strongest role model, but he was not the only person who played the role.

Source: Zizi, 1996, p. 170.

The first relevant text (RT#1) is in L's first response. It is shown, underlined, below.

> L: [The first time I thought about becoming a father was very early in my life. Probably I, I guess because of my upbringing as I was brought up in Church and it was always a serious matter to me. I never went out with a girl without thinking that this is the girl I could possibly marry.]

Our memo for RT#1 reads:

> Being a father is a serious matter, because it is connected with being religious.

The remainder of L's response did not seem to us to contain any more ideas relevant to our research concerns, so we did not underline any other text. If you see another important idea here, it does not mean that you are wrong and we are right. Qualitative research involves an inescapable element of interpretation, and different readers can reasonably disagree. The main issue is that each coder's interpretation must be transparent (understandable) to other coders. We will say more about this when we talk about reliability and validity.

RT#2 occurs in AG's response.

> I was scared to become a father. As a Christian I was afraid not to meet the proper woman to become my wife in order to become a father. When I met my wife and realized that she was a Christian and looking behind at how my father raised us, I decided to become a father at that time.

RT#2 connects being a father with marrying a Christian woman, and therefore with religion. Our memo for RT#2 reads:

> Fatherhood connected with religion

RT#3, also in AG's response, is:

> Fortunately, I had my father as an example I would say. He has been with my mother since I was little, and I would say he is still an example for me.

This expresses the idea that one's own father serves as a model that one strives to emulate. The memo reads:

> One's own father as a model to emulate

RT#4 is in L's second response.

> my father was a very good father. He is a guy who has justice; you cannot make him tremble in front of situations.

The memo reads:

> Expresses his admiration for his father.

This is similar to AG's desire to emulate his father, in RT#3.

Now you should try it. Table 5.4 gives an excerpt from another transcript. Read through the excerpt and do your own underlining for relevant text. When you are finished, compare your selection with ours, which we give in Table 5.5.

Table 5.4
Transcript for You to Underline Relevant Text

Moderator: What did you think it was going to be like?

J: I thought it was going to be an innovative experience. If I could say that, something you actually have the power to influence your personality in a very young mind to do some good. So I think it would be like being from a military background, creating a human being for the profit of society.

C: I could say the moment I met my wife, I thought about being a father. As my first girl friend, I thought eventually I would be married to her. To me it became obvious that I would be a father as a married person. I thought it was going to be a difficult job, a 24-hour job because there is no such thing as part-time fatherhood. I think it takes your whole being mentally and physically. Your presence in the house, in the home is very necessary at all times. My kids—they have it, God bless them they have it. I thought it was going to be a unique experience—you do not learn it in college or anywhere else.

DE: It is on-the-job training.

C: Right!

Moderator: Did you have any role model or reference point?

C: Yes, yes when I think about the days of my youth I can see my father and his dedication. The love that he has shown, and his hard-working style and his honesty. All that left a serious imprint on me. My dream was to look like my father. Everybody saw in him a model. His credibility was something that everybody I would say envies, that type of person he was. They love him—people would give him money to save because they knew he would not spend it. So, I always thought that it would be in my best interest to be like him.

Source: Zizi, 1996, p. 221.

Table 5.5

Our Selections of Relevant Text from Table 5.4

Moderator: What did you think it was going to be like?

J: I thought it was going to be an innovative experience. If I could say that, something you actually have the power to influence your personality in a very young mind to do some good. So I think it would be like being from a military background, creating a human being for the profit of society.

C: I could say the moment I met my wife, I thought about being a father. As my first girl friend, I thought eventually I would be married to her. [To me it became obvious that I would be a father as a married person.] I thought it was going to be a difficult job, a 24-hour job because there is no such thing as part-time fatherhood. I think it takes your whole being mentally and physically. Your presence in the house, in the home is very necessary at all times. My kids—they have it. God bless them they have it. I thought it was going to be a unique experience—you do not learn it in college or anywhere else.

DE: It is on-the-job training.

C: Right!

Moderator: Did you have any role model or reference point?

C: [Yes, yes when I think about the days of my youth I can see my father and his dedication. The love that he has shown, and his hard-working style and his honesty. All that they left a serious imprint on me. My dream was to look like my father.] Everybody saw in him a model. His credibility was something that everybody I would say envies, that type of person he was. They love him—people would give him money to save because they knew he would not spend it. So, I always thought that it would be in my best interest to be like him.

Here is our reading of the second excerpt. We found no relevant text in J's response.

The relevant text in C's response:

To me it became obvious that I would be a father as a married person.

and our corresponding memo:

Being a father is the obvious and natural consequence of marriage.

The short responses of DE and C did not contain relevant text. RT#6 comes from C's next response.

> Yes, yes when I think about the days of my youth I can see my father and his dedication. The love that he has shown, and his hard-working style and his honesty. All that they left a serious imprint on me. My dream was to look like my father.

The memo:

> C admires and desires to emulate his own father.

These ideas were also expressed in RT#3 and RT#4.

6

■ ■ ■ ■ ■ ■ ■ ■ ■

Coding 2: The Mechanics

Phase 2: Hearing What Was Said

IN THIS CHAPTER we will consider the second phase of data analysis, HEARING WHAT WAS SAID. In this phase you will gain more access to the subjective experience of the research participants, by organizing the relevant text into repeating ideas (Step 3) and the repeating ideas into themes (Step 4).

Step 3: Discover Repeating Ideas by Grouping Together Related Passages of Relevant Text

Working on Each Transcript Separately

As you select the relevant text you will notice that different research participants are often expressing the same idea, sometimes with the same or similar words. These are called *repeating ideas.*

A repeating idea is an idea expressed in relevant text by two or more research participants.

Repeating ideas are the beginning building blocks from which you will eventually assemble a theoretical narrative.

In Step 3 you systematically search the selections of relevant text for repeating ideas. You first identify the repeating ideas in each separate transcript (from the focus groups or individual interviews, depending on your methodology). Then you combine the repeating ideas from all of the transcripts into a composite list for the entire research sample. As principal investigator, you first do this by yourself, and then combine your work with that of other coders.

1. Begin by opening the file that contains the list of relevant text for Group 1 (or Individual 1). Then create a new file that will become the list of repeating ideas for Group 1.

2. Now highlight and copy the first selection of relevant text from your relevant text file to your repeating ideas file. We call this first selection the *starter text.*

a. Read through the entire list of relevant text selections, keeping the starter text in mind.
b. Each time you encounter an idea that seems related to the starter text, highlight it and copy it into the repeating idea file. As you do so, you might want to make a note about *how* the two selections of text seem related. If you made memos, move them with the text selections.
c. Read down the list until you have highlighted and moved all the relevant text related to the starter.
d. After you have grouped together all of the selections that seem related to the starter text, return to your original list of relevant text. Highlight and move the first selection of text that you did not group with your original starter text. This new selection becomes your next starter idea, and you then read down the list of relevant text, highlighting and moving all the selections that relate to this starter. You repeat this procedure until you have grouped together as many of your relevant text selections as possible into your repeating idea file.

Table 6.1 gives you an example of a master list of relevant text, and Table 6.2 shows that same text grouped into two repeating ideas.

Table 6.1

Sample List of Relevant Text from the Haitian Father Research

(a) The first time I thought about becoming a father was very early in my life. Probably I, I guess because of my upbringing as I was brought up in Church and it was always a serious matter to me. I never went out with a girl without thinking that, this the girl I could possibly marry. (L, p. 170)

Being a father is a serious matter, because it is connected with being religious.

(b) Fortunately, I had my father as an example I would say. He has been with my mother since I was little, and I would say he is still an example for me. (AG, p. 170)

One's own father as a model to emulate.

(c) My father was a very good father. He is a guy who has justice; you cannot make him tremble in front of situations. (L, p. 170)

Expresses admiration for his father.

(d) I was scared to become a father. As a Christian I was afraid not to meet the proper woman to become my wife in order to become a father. When I met my wife and realized that she was a Christian and looking behind at how my father raised us, I decided to become a father at that time. (AG, p. 170)

Fatherhood connected with religion.

(e) Yes, yes when I think of the days of my youth I can see my father and his dedication. The love that he has shown, and his hard-working style and his honesty. All that they left a serious impression on me. My dream was to look like my father.

Admires and desires to emulate his own father.

(f) To me it became obvious that I would be a father as a married person. (C, p. 221)

Being a father is the obvious and natural consequence of marriage.

Source: Zizi 1996.

Table 6.2

Sample List of Relevant Text Selections Grouped into Repeating Ideas

Haitian fathers
Focus Group 2
Coder: Carl Auerbach — Page 1

Repeating ideas
January 24, 2003

Repeating Idea #1—Something about religion

(a) The first time I thought about becoming a father was very early in my life. Probably I, I guess because of my upbringing as I was brought up in Church and it was always a serious matter to me. I never went out with a girl without thinking that, this is the girl I could possibly marry. (L, p. 170)
Being a father is a serious matter, because it is connected with being religious.
(d) I was scared to become a father. As a Christian I was afraid not to meet the proper woman to become my wife in order to become a father. When I met my wife and realized that she was a Christian and looking behind at how my father raised us, I decided to become a father at that time. (AG, p. 170)
Fatherhood connected with religion.

Repeating Idea #2—Using one's own father as a role model

(b) Fortunately, I had my father as an example I would say. He has been with my mother since I was little, and I would say he is still an example for me. (AG, p. 170)
One's own father as a model to emulate.
(c) My father was a very good father. He is a guy who has justice; you cannot make him tremble in front of situations. (L, p. 170)
Expresses admiration for his father.
(e) Yes, yes when I think of the days of my youth, I can see my father and his dedication. The love that he has shown, and his hard working style and his honesty. All that, they left a serious impression on me. My dream was to look like my father.
Admires and desires to emulate his own father.

Orphan text.

(f) To me it became obvious that I would be a father as a married person. (C, p. 221)
Being a father is the obvious and natural consequence of marriage.

Source: Zizi 1996.

As you can see, in Table 6.2, relevant text (a) was our starter text. We grouped (d) with it because they both related to the importance of religion. In this particular transcript, those were the only text selections related to religion. Thus, after grouping them together, we started again with selection (b) as our new starter text, and looked for other selections to group with it. We grouped selections (b), (c), and (e) together because they related to using their own fathers as positive role models.

We refer to selection (f) as an "orphan" because it does not go together conceptually with any other text selections. After we have grouped together as many relevant text selections from all of the transcripts as possible, we will decide whether to include or discard orphans.

We always use rather pedestrian language to name our repeating ideas when we first group text together, and thus named repeating idea #1 "Something about religion." Then we peruse the text selections looking for an excerpt from the text that we can use as the repeating idea. Using the participants' own words is more evocative of their subjective experience.

In Table 6.2 we underlined two sentences that we eventually used to name the two repeating ideas: 1. "I was brought up in Church and it was always a serious matter to me"; and 2. "My dream was to look like my father." These statements capture the meaning of the text in the fathers' own words. Sometimes you choose the name of a repeating idea as you go through each transcript. You might keep changing the name as you encounter quotes that seem more evocative than your first choice. Sometimes you do not decide on a name until you have gone through all of your transcripts and you have constructed your master list of repeating ideas.

You continue going through your list of relevant text for Group 1 until you have assigned all the relevant text to a repeating idea, or at least as much of it as you can. Because you have highlighted all of the text that you used, you can easily see what text is left over.

Having gotten this far, you will have more of a sense of how the text goes together than you did when you started. Also, several problems may arise, which you can use your newly developed sense of the text to resolve.

Orphans

After you have worked through the list of relevant text, you may be left with some relevant text segments that did not get repeated. You have several choices about what to do with these selections. You can discard the text as unimportant; you can search your transcripts again to try to find text that goes with your solitary text; or you can decide the text is important even if you cannot find other text with which to group it. Sometimes it is important to reflect differences in experience as well as commonalities. Thus, it may be important to report that only one person had a particular experience. Because qualitative research is not focused on quantity, individual differences have an important place in this paradigm.

Ideas Too Broad

When you go back and inspect your list you may find that you have too many items in a group, and can see fine distinctions between items that you originally grouped together. In this case break up your larger group into two smaller groups, each expressing a different repeating idea.

Ideas Too Narrow

Alternatively, you may find that your groups are too small; that you made too many distinctions and have too many ideas. In this case, merge two (or more) groups into a larger one.

Second Thoughts

You may read over your list and find some relevant text that you thought belonged in one place belongs somewhere else. Make the changes. Remember, it's your theory.

When you have worked through the first transcript, create repeating ideas for each of the other transcripts. You may find that the ideas from one group alter your understanding of ideas from the other groups. Make a note of this in your research journal.

Creating Your Master List of Repeating Ideas

3. We now resume the material on page 55. After you have used as much as you can of the relevant text from all of your transcripts, combine the list of repeating ideas for each group into a file that reflects the master list of repeating ideas for the project. Go through this list idea by idea. When ideas are exactly the same, combine them into your final list. If ideas are

similar, combine them as well. In the process you may have to rethink your groupings.

Just as you found orphaned relevant text, you may find a repeating idea in one transcript that does not appear in any of the transcripts of the other groups. Again, you have to make a judgment. If an idea that occurs in only one group seems important for your understanding of the phenomenon, you may decide to keep it. If it does not seem important, discard it. If you do not know what to do, set it aside temporarily and come back to it in later stages of data analysis.

How many repeating ideas should you come up with? There are no hard and fast rules, but we have found that something in the neighborhood of 60 is a workable number, with a minimum of 40 and a maximum of 80. The number that you actually come up with will depend on your cognitive style. If you tend to see fine distinctions everywhere, then your list will probably be large and you will have to reduce it. If you tend to think in broad patterns and see things as similar, then your list will probably be smaller and you will have to expand it. Again, try for about 60 ideas, with the understanding that you can go back and revise if it becomes necessary in later steps.

4. Name your repeating ideas. You may have found evocative quotes to name some of your repeating ideas as you were coding each transcript. Or you may choose the names at the point when you create your master list. Your goal is to choose a short quote that captures the essence of each repeating idea in a dramatic and emotionally vivid way. A good way to find a name is to go through your list and read the relevant text out loud. You may find a phrase that jumps out at you by virtue of its emotional impact, and that will be the name of the repeating idea.

Sometimes you may find that you need to combine two quotes, or give a slight paraphrase. That is fine. If nothing in the text seems to fit, then just give a brief statement of the idea. Remember that you are striving for both emotional impact and accuracy.

For example, we saw in Table 6.2 two repeating ideas composed from relevant text. The first repeating idea, "My dream was to look like my father," expresses how admiration for one's own father leads to a desire to emulate him. The second repeating idea, "I was brought up in Church and it was always a serious matter to me," expresses the connection between religious morality and fatherhood.

The Collaborative Coding Process

We believe that all research should be conducted in groups rather than in isolation, particularly when doing qualitative research. We find that it is ideal to work in groups of four—two students and two more experienced researchers. Each coder goes through the process we have described above. Then the person primarily responsible for the project, the principal investigator, goes over all four sets of coding.

This process makes it more probable that we will not have overlooked any important ideas. Even if one or two of the coders has missed some important repeating ideas, using input from four people usually insures that no important ideas are lost.

After the principal investigator has decided on the repeating ideas from the master list, the results are presented and discussed with the other coders. The other coders may not agree completely with the organization; however, they must be able to see the rationale that the principal investigator used to include each piece of relevant text under each repeating idea. In other words, the organization of the data must be "transparent."

This process often requires that the data be reorganized. As the master list is discussed, someone on the team will undoubtedly identify text that does not reflect the particular repeating idea under which it has been coded. That text segment will then have to be included under a different repeating idea, or discarded altogether. If it is coded elsewhere, including it with other text segments might mean changing the name of a different repeating idea so that it will be inclusive of the new text segment. This reorganizing and refining of the data requires patience.

When you have finished with this phase, congratulate yourself! You have completed the most difficult and labor-intensive part of the coding process. You have immersed yourself in the text, and acquired an enormous familiarity with the text, almost to the point of memorization. This will prove invaluable as you go on to develop theory.

Step 4. Organize Themes by Grouping Repeating Ideas into Coherent Categories

In the next step, you organize the repeating ideas into larger groups that express a common theme.

A theme is an implicit idea or topic that a group of repeating ideas have in common.

For example, a theme in the Haitian father data is:

Praising aspects of the traditional Haitian father

It includes the three repeating ideas:

"My dream was to look like my father."
"There is no inch of laziness in my father."
"I love the way my father treated my mother."

Another theme is:

Dissatisfactions with aspects of traditional Haitian fatherhood

It includes the four repeating ideas:

"My father never said I love you."
"Adults do not play."
"When they say your father is coming, you run inside."
"My father took care of other children and did not care much for me."

These themes are shown in Table B.2 of the Haitian fathers article (see Appendix B). You will follow the same procedure for discovering themes that you used to create your master list of repeating ideas.

1. Begin by opening the file, which contains your master list of repeating ideas. Then open a new file that will be your *themes.*

2. Now direct your attention to the first repeating idea on the printed list, which we will call the *starter idea* for the first theme.

Read through the repeating ideas list, keeping the starter idea in mind. Each time you encounter an idea that seems related to the starter idea, highlight it and copy it onto the theme list. As you do so, make a note of how it seems related to the starter idea (if you like using memos).

Read the list of repeating ideas until you have selected and copied all the repeating ideas similar to the starter, and therefore to each other. In each case, make a note about the conceptual similarities you identified.

Table 6.3

Master List of Repeating Ideas

(a) "My dream was to look like my father."
(b) "My father never said I love you."
(c) "You have to be there whenever the child needs you."
(d) "We are co-workers in the field of God."
(e) "Adults do not play."
(f) "There is no inch of laziness in my father."
(g) "When they say your father is coming, you run inside."
(h) "My father took care of other children and did not much care for me."
(i) "I love the way my father treated my mother."
(j) "You call your kid and say 'I love you.'"

The group of repeating ideas you end up with will define the first theme. The similarities you have recorded in your notes suggest the conceptual basis of the theme.

As an example of how to discover themes, consider the small list of 10 repeating ideas given in Table 6.3. They are the first seven items of Table B.2 in Appendix B, plus three others, given in a scrambled order.

Begin by directing your attention to repeating idea (a) "My dream was to look like my father," which will be the starter for the first theme. Then, keeping (a) in mind, read down the list until you encounter idea (f) "There is no inch of laziness in my father." (a) is similar to (f) in that both express the men's admiration for their own fathers.

Continue reading again until you encounter idea (i) "I love the way my father treated my mother," which expresses the men's admiration for their fathers' behavior toward their mothers, and is therefore similar to the other two. At this point you have come to the end of the list and have discovered the group of repeating ideas that define the first theme. Having selected the repeating ideas for the first theme, highlight and copy them from your list of repeating ideas file into the themes file.

Construct your second theme from the repeating ideas list in the same way. Direct your attention to the first repeating idea that was not included in the first theme. This will be the starter idea for your second theme. Then read through the list, selecting all the repeating ideas similar to the second starter. This group of ideas defines your second theme.

Before you read further, try to construct the second theme, starting with repeating idea (b) "My father never said I love you."

Here's what we did. We began with repeating idea (b) in which the men expressed dissatisfaction with their fathers' absence of affection. We then included repeating idea (e) "Adults do not play," in which the men expressed dissatisfaction with their fathers' being strict, stern figures. Next we included (g) "When they say your father is coming, you run inside," in which the men expressed dissatisfaction about how fearful they were of their fathers. Finally, we included (h) "My father took care of other children and did not much care for me," in which some of the men expressed dissatisfaction that their fathers had children with many women. This group of four repeating ideas defined our second theme.

Continue going through your list of repeating ideas until you have assigned all of them to a theme. Several questions may be occurring to you as you do this exercise. How do you know when repeating ideas are sufficiently similar to express a common theme? How do you know what that theme is?

There is no formula for answering these questions. Some ideas for themes emerge from your literature review. For example, when we read the research on Haitian families in Caribbean journals, we found that the authors described the Haitian father as a remote disciplinarian, and the Haitian husband as someone who frequently had children with women other than their wives. Thus, when the men in our study complained about these aspects of their fathers ("My father never said 'I love you'"), the information was familiar to us. Similarly, we are therapists, so when the men also reported admiring their fathers ("My dream was to look like my father"), we were not surprised that they had both positive and negative feelings about them. We used this conceptual framework of emotional ambivalence, of positive and negative feelings about their fathers, to identify abstract patterns among the repeating ideas.

As you go through the procedure, you will grow to understand the research participants and their subjective world. As this happens, you will find that themes will emerge from the data.

After you have grouped together as many repeating ideas as you can, clear up any loose ends in the same way that you did with the relevant text. Deal with orphans by deleting them, incorporating them into a theme you already have, or going back to your raw text to find more repeating ideas that connect with them. If your themes are too broad or too narrow, make changes accordingly. If you have second thoughts about your list of themes, reorganize it until you are satisfied.

How many themes should you have? Although there is no hard and fast rule, we suggest reducing the number of repeating ideas by a factor of 3 or 4, resulting in from 10 to 20 themes, with an average of 15.

3. The next step in the process is to name your themes. While you were grouping the repeating ideas, you had thoughts about the abstract patterns that pulled those ideas together in your mind. Name the themes with an easily understood phrase that expresses this common thread. Keep these ideas simple, and avoid jargon. The research participants should be able to recognize the themes as something they might have said.

For example, as Table B.2 (Appendix B) in the article shows, we named our first theme *Praising aspects of the traditional Haitian father.* This theme captures how the men admired the way their own fathers fulfilled aspects of the traditional Haitian fathering role.

Similarly, the theme *Dissatisfactions with aspects of traditional Haitian fatherhood* captures how the men were unhappy with some aspects of the traditional Haitian fathering role. Most prominently they were dissatisfied with their fathers' emotional distance and sternness, and wanted to treat their own children differently.

As you struggle with naming your themes, you may decide that your repeating ideas need some revision. It is not unusual at this point to go back and change several repeating ideas and relevant text in order to conform to your new understanding of the data. Many students feel very discouraged when this happens. They thought they had completed the repeating ideas phase and moved on to theme creation. Now they feel as if they are back at square one. If this happens to you, do not lose heart. It is actually a positive step, because it means that you are learning about your participants' subjective experience in a more nuanced way. This is the point of your research!

In our project, we always develop our themes independently and then meet to discuss them as a team. This discussion may result in even more reorganization. Again, we may not ultimately agree on the themes; however, the principle investigator must be able to justify her or his organization to the team.

4. Finally, check your work with a consultant. In our view, this should

be a member of the culture you are studying who is not involved in the research project. In the Haitian fathers study, we used a female psychology graduate student whose family was originally from Haiti, and a Caribbean psychologist who was an expert on cross-cultural research on fathers. In our research on gay fathers, we used two psychologists who were established researchers on gay and lesbian families, both of whom were gay.

Using members of the culture is crucial because of the racism, classism, ethnocentrism, and homophobia that are endemic in our culture. You can either ask your consultants to code a small number of transcripts independently and compare your coding to theirs, or you can bring your organization of the data to the consultant, and ask for feedback. As in previous steps, having to explain and justify your work to someone else will improve your thinking. Make whatever changes result from this discussion, and continue until you and your consultant are satisfied.

7

Coding 2: The Mechanics

Phase 3: Developing Theory

IN THIS CHAPTER we will consider the third phase of data analysis, DEVELOPING THEORY. In this phase you will organize the themes into abstract concepts called theoretical constructs (Step 5), and then use the theoretical constructs to construct a theoretical narrative (Step 6).

Step 5: Develop Theoretical Constructs by Organizing Themes into More Abstract Concepts

The next step is to organize your themes into more abstract groupings that we call theoretical constructs.

> A theoretical construct is an abstract concept that organizes a group of themes by fitting them into a theoretical framework.

Theoretical constructs move the analysis from the description of subjective experience found in repeating ideas and themes to a more abstract and theoretical level. Once you have developed your theoretical constructs you will understand your themes more deeply, because you will see how they fit into a larger theoretical framework.

As an illustration of how theoretical constructs work, consider the theoretical construct BICULTURAL ROLE STRAIN. We will show you how we developed it, but for now just take it as given. BICULTURAL ROLE STRAIN groups together the two themes—*Praising aspects of the traditional Haitian father*, and *Dissatisfactions with aspects of traditional Haitian fatherhood*. Note that the construct does not simply redescribe the two themes, but also fits them into an abstract theoretical framework. It groups the two themes together as displaying the men's internal conflicts about the traditional Haitian fathering role. That is, BICULTURAL ROLE STRAIN describes how the men feel positively about some aspects of the traditional fathering role, and negatively about other aspects.

Developing theoretical constructs will challenge you as a researcher. You are probably used to doing research based on theories taken from the literature and which, therefore, were developed by someone else. In developing theoretical constructs, however, you will have to develop your own theories or apply the theories you already know in a new and creative way. The experience is both difficult and rewarding.

How you use the literature of your field in developing theoretical constructs falls on a continuum.

#1. At one extreme of the continuum, you cannot use much prior research literature because relatively little is known about your sample, or because prior research was biased and simply wrong about the experiences of your participants.

#2. In the middle of the continuum, you do not have a definite body of literature in mind when you analyze your data. However, as you analyze your data you recognize how theories in the literature can be used to make sense of your themes. In this case you use the literature to develop your theoretical constructs.

#3. At the other extreme of the continuum, you begin the research knowing which literature and theoretical constructs you intend to apply to your data. In this case you use your data to elaborate, refine, or validate theories in the literature.

When you investigate a research concern for the first time, you will probably be at level #1 or level #2. That is, after you have collected your data you will be able to use some amount of the theoretical literature to make sense of your findings.

In this chapter, therefore, we will teach you how to bring the literature of your field to bear on the data you have collected. In a later chapter we will cover level #3, in which you use qualitative research to expand and refine specific ideas or theories already in the literature.

The procedure for creating theoretical constructs from themes has the same form as the procedure for creating themes from repeating ideas. However, the mechanics of the process are easier to carry out since you work with a relatively small number of themes. On the other hand, it is more difficult conceptually because you work at a more abstract level.

The steps for developing theoretical constructs from themes are described below. Their numbering corresponds to that for developing themes from repeating ideas.

1. Begin by opening the file that contains your list of themes. Then open a new file for your list of *theoretical constructs.*

2. Now direct your attention to the first theme. This will be the starter theme for the first theoretical construct. Read through the list of themes with the starter theme in mind. Each time you encounter a theme related to the starter, highlight it and copy it into your theoretical constructs file. You should also make a note about the connection between it and the starter. Continue reading down the themes list until you are finished.

The group of themes you end up with defines your first theoretical construct. The connections you have recorded in your notes are clues to the organizing principle for the construct.

Now develop your second theoretical construct from the reduced list in the same way that you developed the first one. Continue in this way until you have worked through the entire list of themes. It is less acceptable to have orphan themes than orphan ideas, which you may have had at an earlier stage. You have already decided that all of the repeating ideas and themes are important. Thus, you must continue to organize your themes until you develop theoretical constructs that include all of them. This may mean that you have to reorganize your repeating ideas into a different set of themes. Again, do not feel discouraged. You are just getting to know your data better.

As an example of how to develop theoretical constructs from themes, consider the list of 5 themes given below. They are the themes from our Haitian fathers paper, assigned a letter of the alphabet for reference. We present them in a scrambled order, so that you may get some sense of the process.

(a) *Praising aspects of the traditional Haitian father*
(b) *An enhanced sense of self*
(c) *Definition of a "good" father*
(d) *God makes all things possible*
(e) *Dissatisfaction with aspects of traditional Haitian fatherhood*

We begin with starter theme (a) *Praising aspects of the traditional Haitian father*. Then we read down the list until we encounter theme (e) *Dissatisfaction with aspects of traditional Haitian fatherhood*, and recognize that (e) goes together with (a), our starter theme. The connection between (a) and (e) is that they both express the men's attitudes toward the traditional Haitian fathering role. In fact, they express conflicting attitudes: (a) shows a positive attitude, and (e) a negative one. We record this observation in our notes, to be used when we are ready to name the first theoretical construct.

At this point we have gone through the working list of themes, and have discovered the group of themes that define the first theoretical construct.

The remaining themes on our list were:

(b) *An enhanced sense of self*
(c) *Definition of a "good" father*
(d) *God makes all things possible*

The starter theme for our second theoretical construct was (b) *An enhanced sense of self*. We read down the list until we encountered (c) *Definition of a "good" father*, and grouped (c) with (b). The connection between (b) and (c) is that they are both concerned with reconstructing the traditional Haitian fathering role. Theme (c) describes features of the reconstructed role and theme (b) describes the enhanced sense of self that resulted from enacting the new role. These observations were used in naming the second theoretical construct.

At this point we have finished reading through the list of themes, and discovered the themes that define our second theoretical construct.

In our case, we had an additional theme, (d) *God makes all things possible.* We kept this theme on our final list because we thought the issue of religion was of theoretical importance, even if we only had one theme to support it. Were we to do the data analysis again, knowing what we know now, we would have gone back to our data and created other themes to go with it.

3. Name your theoretical constructs. When you were grouping the themes you had thoughts about the organizing principles that hold the themes in each group together. Now you have to draw on the literature and your general knowledge to find a theory or concept that explains this organizing principle. The name of the theoretical construct should use the language of the theory on which you draw.

At this point your theoretical framework begins to organize the data in a very concrete way. Our social constructionist framework led us to think about gender roles from a gender role strain paradigm, originally developed by Joe Pleck (1981). This paradigm proposed that definitions of masculinity and femininity are constructed by cultural ideology, rather than by biological givens. As men and women try to conform to these cultural norms, they experience a great deal of psychological strain because the norms are rigid, and often contradictory. For example, masculinity ideology requires men to be both aggressive in their professional lives and emotionally responsive to their families. The strain paradigm proposed that it is stressful for young boys to develop both the empathy required to be emotionally responsive in intimate relationships and the ruthlessness necessary to be physically and professionally aggressive.

When we listened to the Haitian fathers talk about having both positive and negative feelings about their fathers, we immediately thought about how having both sets of feelings would generate emotional stress in the men. This made us think about the gender role strain paradigm.

We also knew a little bit about acculturation theory at this point. We knew that immigrants experience strain as they attempt to integrate both their culture of origin and the host country's culture. We thought that the first group of themes reflected ambivalent *personal* feelings about their fathers, as well as a conflict between two cultural models of fatherhood: the traditional Haitian fathering role, and the nurturant fathering role they were exposed to in the United States. Thus, we merged the concepts of gender role strain and acculturation strain into the theoretical construct of BICULTURAL GENDER ROLE STRAIN.

In retrospect, we have come to believe that the theoretical construct of role strain is particularly relevant to the way that all men are experiencing transformations in the fathering role, and therefore we have developed it further in our later work.

We did less well with a name for the theoretical construct that comprised the two themes *Definition of a "good" father* and *An enhanced sense of self*. We named the theoretical construct CONSTRUCTING A MORE GRATIFYING DEFINITION OF FATHERHOOD. This name, which is not very abstract or theoretical, simply describes how the two themes fit together.

Our research concern was to understand how men could change from defining fathering almost exclusively in terms of providing financial resources to his family, to becoming more emotionally connected fathers. Thus, we were thinking about theories of change. As psychologists, we were trained in behavior modification theory which has shown that positive reinforcement is the most effective way to change behavior. Therefore, we assumed that in order to change an old role, men had to define for themselves a new and more gratifying role. We saw the theme *Definition of a "good" father* as describing the new role the men defined for themselves, and saw the theme *An enhanced sense of self* as describing the satisfaction (positive reinforcement) they derived from enacting the new role. In retrospect, we would have grouped these themes somewhat differently.

At this stage in our study of fathering, we also began to develop a general theoretical model for how roles change. We were already thinking of the construct of ROLE STRAIN as describing the necessary motivation for change. By this we meant that an individual must feel some kind of stress or dissatisfaction with his behavior in order to be motivated to change. Contemporary research on fathers had documented how emotionally isolated fathers felt from family life (Snarey, 1993). We also had incorporated the idea that a person had to have some reinforcement for making the change. This was reflected in the construct, DEFINING A MORE GRATIFYING ROLE. LaRossa (1997) and others have described how the nurturing father role offers men a sense of intimacy and emotional connection with their children that many men find rewarding.

We began to ask ourselves what else had to be present in order for role change to occur, and hypothesized two additional constructs: FACILITATING IDEOLOGY and SOCIAL SUPPORT. FACILITATING IDEOLOGY described a set of beliefs from which the new role was constructed. Ideology prescribes the behavior associated with the new role. SOCIAL SUPPORT described support from others in coping with the difficulties and anxieties associated with adopting a new role.

We had no definite thematic support for either of our hypothesized constructs. However, they made sense to us and we included the orphaned theme *God makes all things possible* as tentative support for FACILITATING IDEOLOGY. In addition, we made a note to ourselves to pursue both new constructs in our future research. We will say more about this when we discuss research aimed at developing preexisting theory.

4. Finally, as before, verify your work with consultants, and make whatever changes emerge from the feedback they give you. In our case, we spoke with a Haitian student at Yeshiva University who helped us understand the change of the fathering role better. We also spoke with a colleague, JaiPaul Roopnarine, who helped us explicitly connect our work to the more general topic of immigration and acculturation.

Step 6: Create a Theoretical Narrative by Retelling the Participant's Story in Terms of Theoretical Constructs

In the sixth and final step, you pull together all the work you have done so far in order to address the research concerns that led to your study. You do this with a device called a theoretical narrative.

> A theoretical narrative describes the process that the research participants reported in terms of your theoretical constructs. It uses your theoretical constructs to organize people's subjective experience into a coherent story. It employs people's own language to make their story vivid and real.

The process of data analysis is so comprehensive that by the time you reach this stage, you probably have almost memorized the text. However, when we are "organizing data," we often become too abstract and theoretical. You have spent a great deal of time attempting to make sure that each relevant text segment actually reflects the repeating idea under which it is coded and that all of the repeating ideas actually relate conceptually to the way you organized the themes. Paradoxically, this emphasis on consistency and organization may have caused you to lose touch with the participants' subjective experience. Creating the theoretical narrative will cause the text to come alive for you, and you will understand the research participants and their lives even better. In addition, you will integrate the subjective world of people's experience with the abstract world of theory.

You create a theoretical narrative by organizing your constructs into a *personal story* that describes the subjective experience of your research participants. In this way it contrasts with more traditional research conclusions that are usually written from a more distant, "scientific" stance.

We will illustrate how to write a theoretical narrative by interspersing our instructions with excerpts from the Haitian father narrative. This should make the abstract instructions more comprehensible.

1. Begin your theoretical narrative by describing your research concerns.

> When our Haitian American research participants were thinking about becoming fathers, and when they became fathers, they had to decide what sort of father they wanted to be. Naturally, they had their own father in mind in making this decision. Here is the story of how it happened.

2. Then describe your first theoretical construct as it applies to your research participants. Break down the construct into its thematic experiential components, using the language of the repeating ideas to make the experience vivid and real. Using the repeating ideas tells the story in your participants' own words. We put the theoretical constructs and the themes in parentheses directly in the narrative so that the reader can see clearly how we are grounding the narrative in the data. Also, we put the repeating ideas in quotes, because they represent the research participant's own words.

> The decision about what kind of father they wanted to be was difficult because they felt conflicted about their own father (BICULTURAL GENDER ROLE STRAIN). On the onc hand, there was a lot about him that they admired (*Praising aspects of the traditional Haitian father*). They admired how responsible, hard working and strong he was: "There was no inch of laziness

> in him." Some of them admired how good a husband he was, and "loved the way he treated their mother." For these reasons, they wanted to be like their father: "Their dream was to look like their father."
>
> On the other hand, there were aspects of their father that they did not like (*Dissatisfaction with aspects of traditional Haitian fatherhood*). They did not like how emotionally distant he was; how "he never said I love you." Nor did they like his strictness: "When they heard that their father was coming, they ran inside." Also they were troubled by his sternness; as the saying has it, "adults do not play." Some of them were troubled by the fact that their fathers had children from multiple marriages: "Took care of other children and did not care much for me."

3. Do this for each of the constructs. When you are done you will have told the research participants' story in terms of both their own words and the theoretical constructs.

The narrative style should talk about the research participants in the third person (they), and be addressed to a literate academic audience, not necessarily to specialists in your field. It may help you get into people's experience if you initially write the narrative in the first person (I), and then later convert it into the third person.

This completes our theoretical narrative for the first construct. Now we do the same thing for the second construct, CONSTRUCTING A MORE GRATIFYING DEFINITION OF FATHERHOOD. You might want to try doing this yourself before reading our description.

> When they became a father, they wanted to be a father in a new way, one that was more gratifying than the old way (CONSTRUCTING A MORE GRATIFYING DEFINITION OF FATHERHOOD).
>
> They defined what it meant to be a good father by keeping what they liked about the old role and changing the rest (*Definition of a "good" father*). They wanted to do what their fathers did; to look after the family, to be a provider and protector. However, they wanted to be less authoritarian, "less like a boss to their children and more like a friend." Also, they wanted to be more emotionally connected and demonstrative, less strict and stern. They wanted to "be there when the child needed them," and "always say 'I love you.'"
>
> When they tried to imagine how to be a loving father, they thought about

> Jesus as a loving image of God. This identification with Jesus helped them to become a more affectionate and emotionally connected father: "Jesus was my role model."
>
> The result of being a father was that they grew as a person (*An enhanced sense of self*). They were changed, reconstructed as a more responsible adult. They also derived enormous pleasure from being a father: "I watched my children grow and it was beautiful."

The theoretical narrative concludes your study and also points you toward the next study. It summarizes where your research has taken you, leads you to reformulate your theoretical framework and research concerns, and focuses your attention on what you are not yet clear about.

In our case, the theoretical narrative moved us from the somewhat general research concern with the subjective experience of fatherhood to the more definite concern with how men are redefining the fathering role. It gave us a conceptual framework in terms of the four theoretical constructs. Finally, it set us on a new path, of elaborating our constructs by a process of theoretical sampling.

8

■ ■ ■ ■ ■ ■ ■ ■ ■

Convincing Other People

The Issues Formerly Known as Reliability, Validity, and Generalizability

YOU HAVE JUST USED our data analysis procedure to construct a theoretical narrative. How should you evaluate the work you have done? Qualitative and quantitative methodologies answer this question differently.

Quantitative methodology tries to exclude subjectivity, interpretation, and context from scientific practice. It requires that data analysis procedures be "objective" and that theories be universally applicable. The requirements of objectivity and universality are translated into statistical concepts. Objectivity corresponds to the statistical concepts of *reliability and validity*, and universality corresponds to the statistical concept of *generalizability.*

As qualitative researchers we strongly disagree with the quantitative approach to evaluating research. We believe, instead, that subjectivity, interpretation, and context are inevitably interwoven into every research project. Furthermore, we believe that these elements of research practice are essential and should not be eliminated even if it were possible to do so. However, we agree with quantitative methodologists that standards for evaluating research are essential. We do not think that qualitative research is an area in which "anything goes."

In this chapter we will recommend standards for evaluating research that are consistent with the qualitative research paradigm, and therefore take into account subjectivity, interpretation, and context. In place of the quantitative concepts of reliability and validity, we suggest the qualitative concept of *justifiability of interpretations*. In place of the quantitative concept of generalizability we suggest the qualitative concept of *transferability of theoretical constructs*. You should know, however, that there are many different qualitative approaches to these issues. For alternatives to ours, you can consult Smith and Deemer (2000).

Pursuing the Unreachable Ideal: A Skeptical Look at Reliability, Validity, and Generalizability

When you studied the concepts of reliability, validity, and generalizability in statistics or research design courses, they were probably presented to you in the language of mathematics and statistical theory. Such a formal presentation is certainly necessary for learning how to do statistical computations. In focusing on the mathematical details, however, students often lose sight of the philosophical issues involved in these concepts. Because it is precisely the philosophical issues that we want to explore, we will deal with the concepts simply, without the mathematical details.

In the discussion that follows, we are going to assert that more is claimed for the statistical tools of reliability, validity, and generalizability than they actually deliver. We will show you that these tools can work only in an ideal situation that does not, and indeed cannot, obtain in practice.

The Trouble with Reliability and Validity

Reliability and validity are important criteria for evaluating quantitative research because they are intended to assure the reader that the measuring scales are objective. Objectivity is difficult to define precisely; generations of philosophers have devoted their lives to the task with no end to their labors in sight. For our purposes, however, the definition is straightforward: Objectivity simply means the absence of subjectivity. If our measuring scales are objective then we are studying the phenomenon as it really is, excluding our subjective biases about what we would like it to be.

What is the connection between objectivity, reliability, and validity? We begin considering this question by defining reliability. The way to determine whether a scale is reliable is to administer it twice. If the numerical score you get from the second administration of the scale is the same, or almost the same, as the numerical score you got from the first administration, then the measure is reliable. Conversely, if the numerical scores on the first and second administrations are wildly different, then the scale is not reliable. For example, if you measure satisfaction with fathering and get a value of 7 the first time and a value of 6.5 the second, then the satisfaction with fathering scale is reliable. But if the first value is 7 and the second value is 2, then the scale is not reliable.

The reliability of a scale is a *necessary* condition for the scale to be objective. If you get a value of 7 the first time you measure something, and a value of 2 the second time you measure it, you clearly do not know the true value of what you are measuring. If you have no understanding of a response's true value, you are free to impose your subjectivity on it, and to say that its value is whatever you would like it to be.

However, the reliability of a scale is not a *sufficient* condition for the scale to be objective. Imagine, for example, the "measurement task" of asking someone the question "How are you?" The first time you take the measurement (i.e., ask the question), they respond "fine." The second time you take the measurement, they also respond "fine." Your "scale" is clearly reliable, because you got the same "measurement value" when you administered it both times. However, the reliability of the answer hardly proves that the person is indeed fine. It is equally likely that he is simply being polite.

For a scale to be objective it must not only be reliable, it must also be *valid*. A scale is defined as valid if it measures what it claims to measure. Thus, a scale of satisfaction with fatherhood is valid if it measures how satisfied fathers *really* are, as distinct from how satisfied they *say* they are. (Many texts distinguish between different kinds of validity—face validity, construct validity, predictive validity—but for our purposes we will stick with the basic definition.) The fact that a scale is valid proves that it is objective, because if the scale measures what it claims to be measuring, then your subjective desires will not influence the value of the measurement.

The problem with validity arises when we consider how we might determine whether a scale measures what it claims to be measuring, and is therefore valid. To appreciate the problem, imagine that you are doing research on satisfaction with fatherhood. While planning your research, you discover that there is no scale for measuring father satisfaction and so develop your own. Having developed your scale, you need to prove that it is valid. How might you do this? To prove that your newly developed scale of fatherhood satisfaction is valid, you must compare the results of your scale with the true value of father satisfaction. However, you do not know the true value! In order to know the true value you would have to already possess a valid scale, but a valid scale is precisely what you are trying to develop. It would seem that there is no way to develop a valid scale for the first time, for what would you validate it against?

We refer to this problem with reliability and validity as "pursuing the unreachable ideal." The phrase is intended to express the idea that developing a first valid scale requires comparing it with another valid scale, and that this second valid scale must have been developed by comparing it with a third already valid scale, and so on to infinity. Because of this problem, we suggest that you be skeptical about the concept of validity in the social sciences.

The Trouble with Generalizability

Generalizability is an important criterion for evaluating quantitative research because it is intended to assure the person who reads the research report that the theory derived from the research is universally applicable. A universally applicable theory is one that applies to everyone in the population you are concerned with, and is not dependent on idiosyncratic characteristics of the people you used to develop the theory. This is important for people who want to use the research. If they know the theory is universally applicable, then they can apply it to new situations with confidence.

Before going further, we must define the concept of *representative sampling*. The definition applies to research in which an investigator wants to learn about an entire population, but is not able to study all of it. Instead, he studies only a group of people selected from the population—a sample. His sample is representative of the population if the distribution of characteristics of the sample is the same as that of the population. Clearly, the investigator must obtain a representative sample if he wants to develop a generalizable, universally applicable theory.

As an illustration of these concepts, imagine that we do a study to investigate whether fathers in the United States are more likely to relate well to their sons or to their daughters. (We use this example only to make a point. We would not do this type of research because we do not think generalizations like this are helpful to understanding the subjective experience of the individual.)

The population we are concerned with is all U.S. fathers. Despite our interest in all U.S. fathers, our time and money are limited, so we sample a large group of New York fathers from a variety of ethnic groups and socioeconomic classes. These fathers, we discover, all on average, prefer sons and daughters equally. What can we conclude from this study? Clearly, our sample is unlikely to be representative of all the fathers in the United States, since New York fathers probably differ from fathers in other parts of the country in important ways. Because we did not obtain a representative sample, we cannot generalize our results and develop general theory. It is quite possible that rural, Midwestern farming fathers, unlike New York fathers, do prefer their sons to their daughters.

This situation is unsatisfactory. Researchers want to develop generalizable theories, so they must be able to prove that their samples are representative. However, a problem arises when they try to do so, a problem similar to the one arising with validity. To appreciate the problem, imagine that you have done a study of Haitian fathers and find that the fathers *in your sample* prefer their sons to their daughters. How can you determine whether your results are generalizable? To determine this you must prove that you have a representative sample. That is, you must rule out the possibility that you inadvertently selected a research sample with some special characteristics, or that your results were produced by some special factor or circumstances of which you are unaware.

But how can you rule out these possibilities? This is where the problem arises. In order to assure yourself that you have a representative sample, you must do your study with a second, larger sample and see if you get the same results as you did the first time. However, even getting the same results will not settle the matter, because the same question can be asked about the second, larger sample. For example, we could include Midwestern farming fathers in the second sample, but those results might not apply to Hawaiian fathers or Alaskan fathers. This will lead you to study a third, even larger sample, and so forth.

Ultimately, the logic of the argument requires that you study every conceivable Haitian father in every conceivable relevant circumstance. This requirement is, of course, impossible to meet. Just as with validity, proving that your results are generalizable involves you in the pursuit of an unreachable ideal. Thus, we suggest that you be skeptical about the concept of generalizability.

Why Doesn't Everyone Say This?

At this point, you might be wondering why, if our criticisms are correct, people still use the concepts of reliability, validity, and generalizability. Statisticians would respond to our criticisms by admitting that our points are correct, but would argue that we exaggerate their importance. They would admit, in connection with validity, that the true score is a hypothetical abstract entity that is inferred, rather than directly observed. They would similarly admit, in connection with generalizability, that the population is inferred, rather than directly observed. Where we part company with the statisticians is that they believe the inferences are valid, whereas we consider them unjustified.

We do not ask you to accept our argument uncritically. Indeed, if you have the inclination, you should look into these issues further and make up your own mind. What we do ask of you is to recognize that reliability, validity, and generalizability are not completely solid guarantees of trustworthy research in the social sciences. Rather, they require you to accept assumptions that are not immediately self-evident and are, in fact, somewhat problematic. Having persuaded you of at least this much, we ask that you be open to the idea that qualitative research can be as trustworthy as quantitative research.

Don't Throw the Baby Out with the Bathwater Part 1: Justifiability as an Alternative to Reliability and Validity

Although we have just cautioned you about making too much of reliability and validity, we believe that quantitative researchers are right to insist on distinguishing between justified and unjustified application of our subjectivity. We think it is justifiable, even inevitable, for a researcher to *use* his subjectivity in analyzing and interpreting data. However, it is not justifiable for him to *impose* his own subjectivity in an arbitrary manner, that is, in a way that is not grounded in the data. Unjustifiable use of subjectivity is, in effect, interpreting data based on the researcher's prejudices and biases, without regard to the participants' experience.

Here are examples of justifiable and unjustifiable uses of subjectivity in interpretation. From our feminist perspective, the Haitian fathers in our studies were expressing their dissatisfaction with some aspects of traditional masculinity in terms of the way in which it is prescribed in the traditional fathering role. Although this interpretation is influenced by our subjective, feminist perspective, we nevertheless regard it as justified, because it is based on data.

For example, traditional masculinity ideology requires men to be stoic and emotionally inexpressive. The Haitian fathers described their fathers as emotionally distant disciplinarians who never played with them. They complained that their fathers never said "I love you." We see these statements as two examples of the way that traditional masculinity was expressed in the traditional Haitian fathering role. The men in our study, unlike their fathers, stated that they wanted to be "friends" to their children, and to tell them often that they loved them.

We might have gone further in our interpretation and claimed that the men in our study were repudiating all aspects of traditional masculinity. This perspective matches our bias because we believe that traditional masculinity has negative consequences for both men and women. However, nothing in the data suggested that the Haitian fathers were rejecting traditional masculinity altogether. Rather, some data suggested that there were certain aspects of traditional masculinity that the men embraced.

For example, several of the men referred to themselves as "gods within their families." This perspective reflects the male dominance explicit in traditional masculinity ideology. If we had suggested that the men were relinquishing a commitment to male dominance, we would have been imposing our subjective desires on the data, thereby distorting the experience of our research participants.

Consequently, we need criteria for distinguishing between justifiable and unjustifiable ways of using subjectivity to interpret data. The criteria that we use are called transparency, communicability, and coherence (Rubin & Rubin, 1995). Each of these criteria involves making use of other people to check against the tendency to impose one's own subjective biases on the data analysis.

Transparency

For your data analysis to be justifiable it must be *transparent*. This means that other researchers can know the steps by which you arrived at your interpretation. It does not mean that other researchers need to agree with your interpretation; only that they know how you arrived at it. This book is aimed at making our data analysis procedure transparent. If you follow our steps, and keep a record of what you have done, you are guaranteed to produce a transparent analysis.

As an example of transparency, consider our theoretical construct of BICULTURAL GENDER ROLE STRAIN. We have shown you how it was built up out of two themes: *Praising aspects of traditional Haitian fatherhood*, and *Dissatisfaction with traditional Haitian fatherhood*. We have shown you, too, how these themes were built up out of repeating ideas, which in turn were derived from relevant text. At each step of the process, we explained our procedure, so that you could know exactly what we did.

You may not agree that our organization of the data is the best framework for understanding the Haitian fathers that we studied. However, you can see how we arrived at our organizational framework. We hope you will agree that the relevant text segments are included within the appropriate repeating ideas; that the repeating ideas are grouped into themes in an understandable way; and that the theoretical constructs correctly identify patterns among the themes. If our interpretation of the data is transparent, it means that it is justifiable; that we did not simply make it up to suit ourselves.

Communicability

For your data analysis to be justifiable it must also be *communicable*. This means that your themes and constructs can be understood by, and make sense to, other researchers, and to the research participants themselves.

Again, this does not mean that other researchers would have come up with your constructs, or agree with them. It only means that what you have done can be understood.

You can determine whether your themes and theoretical constructs are communicable by trying to explain them, and seeing if you succeed. You do this by describing it to other researchers and to your research participants. If they understand what you are saying, then the construct is communicable. If they do not, then you must go back to the drawing board.

Using the Haitian fathers as an example, we know that our construct of BICULTURAL GENDER ROLE STRAIN is communicable because we have successfully explained it, both to other researchers and to our research participants. Other researchers recognized instances of role strain in their own lives, and because we have based our work on the participants' own words, they can understand the experience of our research participants. When we described our theoretical constructs to the research participants themselves, again because we used their own words as much as possible, they recognized themselves in what we said about them and acknowledged that we captured their experience.

Coherence

For your data analysis to be justifiable, it must be *coherent*. This means that your theoretical constructs must fit together and allow you to tell a coherent story. This does not require that the story you develop be the only possible one, but rather that your story helps to organize the data. Our data analysis procedure helps you produce coherent ideas by developing constructs that fit into an organized theoretical narrative

For example, our two theoretical constructs, BICULTURAL ROLE STRAIN and CONSTRUCTING A MORE GRATIFYING DEFINITION OF FATHERHOOD, fit together into an organized narrative that describes how the men reconstructed the traditional Haitian fathering role. In this case, the two theoretical constructs are reciprocally related. The role strain is the motivation for constructing a more gratifying definition of fatherhood; and the more gratifying definition reduces the tension associated with role strain. At this point, it may help you to reread the theoretical narrative in chapter 7 to see, in more detail, how the two constructs fit together.

Don't Throw the Baby Out with the Bathwater Part 2: Transferability as an Alternative to Generalizability

Our point about reliability and validity also holds true for generalizability. We think that quantitative methodology is wrong to insist that theories be generalizable and universally applicable. Indeed, this criterion led quantitative methodology to ignore gender differences and cultural diversity. However, we think that quantitative methodology is right to insist that theories be applicable to people other than the particular sample on which they were developed. The question is how to balance the two requirements of simultaneously extending beyond your sample and respecting cultural diversity. It seems impossible to do both at the same time; the two requirements seem incompatible.

For example, although the Haitian fathers in our sample experienced *bicultural* gender role strain, it seems unlikely that fathers born in the United States will experience the same kind of bicultural gender role strain. This would seem to imply that our results are applicable only to Haitian fathers. In other words, in our efforts to respect cultural diversity, we developed a form of role strain so specific to Haitian fathers that it cannot be extended to any other group.

These two requirements are not really incompatible because different levels of grounded theory analysis do different things. The more abstract level of theoretical constructs extends beyond the sample, whereas themes and repeating ideas are culturally specific. Thus, we do not expect fathers born in the United States to experience *bicultural* gender role strain in the same way that the Haitian fathers did. However, because the issue of gender role strain is a more general one, we do expect fathers born in the United States to experience some sort of role strain. Not surprisingly, we have found BICULTURAL GENDER ROLE STRAIN in Latino immigrant fathers, although the content of that strain was somewhat different than the strain that the Haitian fathers were experiencing.

Thus, the theoretical construct of role strain potentially extends beyond the sample of Haitian fathers; whereas the themes and repeating ideas, the *specifics* of the role strain, vary from culture to culture. In this way, it is possible for theory developed within a qualitative design to extend beyond a specific sample and also to be culturally specific.

We need a term to describe theoretical constructs that can be extended beyond a particular sample and yet respect cultural diversity. We do not want to call them generalizable, because that term does not quite capture what we are after. The term we will use is *transferable.* The theoretical constructs you develop in grounded theory are transferable, in that you can expect the more abstract patterns that they describe to be found in different subcultures. The specific content of those patterns, in contrast, will depend on the specific subculture being studied.

If a construct is truly transferable, it will serve as a guide for investigating a new sample. When you try to apply a theoretical construct to the new sample, you should find that the theoretical constructs you developed in one study will help you understand the subjective experiences of the participants in the new sample. However, the constructs usually do not apply automatically. As you try to apply the constructs you will also find yourself extending their meaning and developing them further. This is an example of theoretical sampling. As you include more samples, you refine theory.

For example, when we began studying Promise Keeper fathers, we assumed that the role strain construct developed with the Haitian fathers was transferable, and therefore would apply to the Promise Keepers. Our goal was to understand specifics of role strain in the Promise Keepers, and to compare it with the role strain that the Haitian fathers were experiencing. We will develop this point further in the next chapter, in which we discuss our research with the Promise Keeper fathers.

DESIGNING AND ANALYZING YOUR NEXT RESEARCH STUDY

Part IV

9

■ ■ ■ ■ ■ ■ ■ ■ ■

Designing Your Next Study Using Theoretical Sampling

The Promise Keeper Fathers

IN THE PREVIOUS CHAPTER, we proposed that theory developed in the context of a specific sample could extend beyond that sample to apply to other sample populations. After you have completed your first research study, you will have to deal with the following question.

> The theory that you developed in your first research study is applicable only to the research sample from that study. How do you further develop your theory so that it is useful for understanding other research samples?

This is what we call the *transferability question*. As you will recall from chapter 8, the qualitative concept of transferability roughly corresponds to the quantitative concept of generalizability. In doing qualitative research, you try to develop transferable theories. This means that the *abstract patterns* described by your theoretical constructs will be applicable to other research samples, even though their *specific content* will not be.

Here is how the transferability question can be stated for the role strain construct that we developed in the Haitian Fathers Study.

> How does the role strain construct that emerged from our particular research sample apply to other groups of Haitian fathers, and to other subcultures of fathers?

The question, then, is how to develop the theory from your first research study into a more transferable theory. There are two distinct issues.

1. How do you design your next study (or sequence of studies) in order to develop your theory further?
2. How do you analyze the data from your next study (or sequence of studies) in order to develop your theory further?

Designing your next study will be the topic of this chapter, and analyzing the data from your next study will be the topic of the following chapter. Our discussion of the design question will focus on strategies for selecting a new research sample, using the method of theoretical sampling. After we explain theoretical sampling, we will present five steps for designing your next study.

As in previous chapters, we will illustrate the methodology with material drawn from the Yeshiva University Fatherhood Project. In particular we will describe the study that we published after the Haitian Fathers Study, which investigated fathers involved in the Promise Keepers, a fundamentalist Christian movement. The original paper describing this work is included as Appendix C (Silverstein, Auerbach, Grieco, & Dunkel, 1999). You should read through it at this point.

Theoretical Sampling

What Is Theoretical Sampling?

The method for selecting a research sample for your next study is called theoretical sampling.

> Theoretical sampling is the process of choosing a research sample in order to extend and refine a theory.

The Haitian Fathers Study provides an illustration of the need for theoretical sampling. In that study, we described Haitian fathers' subjective experience of fatherhood in terms of two theoretical constructs for which we had extensive textual evidence: BICULTURAL GENDER ROLE STRAIN, and CONSTRUCTING A MORE GRATIFYING DEFINITION OF FATHERHOOD. In addition, we developed two other theoretical constructs: RELIGIOUS FACILITATING IDEOLOGY, and SOCIAL SUPPORTS. We had less solid textual evidence for these two constructs.

The goals of our next study, the Promise Keepers Study, were to discover whether these theoretical constructs could be extended beyond the Haitian fathers sample, and if so, to gather more textual evidence to support them. We used theoretical sampling to achieve these goals.

Differences Between Random Sampling and Theoretical Sampling

Table 9.1 summarizes the differences between theoretical sampling and random sampling. The differences reflect the contrast between qualitative and quantitative approaches to scientific knowledge.

To uncover the differences, consider this question about our Haitian Fathers Study: What useful knowledge about fathers can come from a single study that uses a convenience sample of 22 self-selected fathers from a particular religious community in Brooklyn, New York? One very natural answer is: "Not much useful knowledge at all. Your study only describes those 22 men."

Both the random sampling perspective and the theoretical sampling perspective agree that more research needs to be done before one can

Table 9.1

Differences Between Random Sampling and Theoretical Sampling

	Random Sampling	Theoretical Sampling
Goals	Generalizable propositions about a population	Transferable constructs about a research concern
Methods for achieving goals	Representative sampling from that population	In-depth exploration of constructs in different contexts
Method for selecting sample size	Statistical power analysis	Theoretical saturation

assume that the theory developed from this study is applicable to other groups of fathers. However, these two approaches disagree about why, and what sorts of research. To illustrate the differing approaches, we will focus on the theoretical construct of BICULTURAL GENDER ROLE STRAIN.

As Table 9.1 shows, the goal of random sampling is to develop general propositions about a particular population on the basis of a representative sample from that population. Such general propositions might be: All Haitian fathers experience bicultural role strain; or, All fathers, Haitian or not, experience role strain.

From the random sampling perspective, the Haitian father study is clearly not adequate.

1. The 22 Haitian fathers represent only themselves. Because the sample is small and self-selected, they are not a representative sample of Haitian fathers, and even less are they a representative sample of all fathers.
2. Therefore, no useful knowledge can be obtained from conclusions drawn from this sample alone.

Thus, the random sampling perspective would make the following recommendation for further research.

> In order to obtain a more representative sample, replicate the research study using a greater variety of fathers, both Haitian fathers and fathers in general. Make sure not to use a self-selected sample.

From the theoretical sampling perspective, the Haitian Fathers Study looks quite different.

1. The theoretical sampling perspective agrees that the 22 fathers represent only themselves.
2. Despite this, however, useful knowledge has come from the study. The construct of BICULTURAL GENDER ROLE STRAIN was developed from the sample, and the construct itself is useful. We felt safe in concluding that this construct is useful because gender role strain is a concept that has emerged from research in the field of men's studies (Pleck, 1995). Gender role strain was originally de-

veloped in terms of masculine gender role socialization. It spoke, in general, to the issue of developing a masculine gender role identity. However, it did not address how the strain was experienced in the specific roles that men fulfill. Our study illustrated how gender role strain was experienced in particular, in terms of the fathering role. In addition, our study showed how conflicting cultural gender role prescriptions cause strain in the life of immigrant fathers. Thus, our concept of BICULTURAL GENDER ROLE STRAIN extends and develops Pleck's concept.

3. However, our understanding of the construct needs to be developed further in order to determine whether other men are experiencing role strain in their fathering role, and whether cultural aspects of role strain can also be found in the subjective experience of other immigrant fathers.

Therefore, the theoretical sampling perspective makes the following recommendations for further research.

> Investigate the construct of role strain in a variety of different contexts. The purpose is not to achieve generalizability, but to understand the construct further. The new investigations will be based on what we learned from the first study, rather than simply replicating it.

Both the random sampling perspective and the theoretical sampling perspective lead us to study further research samples, but for different reasons and in different ways. Random sampling aims at generalizability, and would lead us to try to obtain a more representative sample. Theoretical sampling aims at elaborating the theoretical construct further, and so would choose research samples geared to that end.

Strategies for Theoretical Sampling

Table 9.2 describes six basic strategies for doing theoretical sampling. Note that these strategies are not exclusive; the same research sample may be an application of more than one strategy. We will describe these strategies and indicate how they might have been used to select our next research sample.

Table 9.2

Six Strategies for Theoretical Sampling to Further Develop a Theoretical Construct

Theoretical Sampling Strategy	Purpose
Convenience sampling	To obtain information about your theoretical construct in a convenient fashion
Extreme or unusual case sampling	To obtain information about extreme or unusual examples of your theoretical construct
Central or critical case sampling	To obtain information about situations where your theoretical construct is assumed to be present
Typical or paradigm case sampling	To obtain information about your theoretical construct in everyday life
Similar case sampling	To obtain information about how your theoretical construct operates in a range of situations similar to your original study
Sensitive or political case sampling	To obtain information about how your theoretical construct operations in situations in the public eye

Convenience Sampling

The method of convenience sampling was discussed in chapter 2. The basic idea is to choose a research sample to which you have easy and immediate access. This strategy makes the assumption that any information obtained from the convenience sample will be informative.

In our case, we let our graduate students choose their samples because they were the ones collecting the data. We wanted them to choose the samples that were most convenient for them.

Extreme or Unusual Case Sampling

The strategy of extreme or unusual case sampling involves choosing a research sample in which you expect your theoretical construct to be present in an extreme or unusual way.

Possible extreme case samples relevant to role strain are gay fathers, stay-at-home fathers, and single fathers. We expect role strain to be present in an extreme way in these cases because each of them requires men to be fathers without a mother at home to assume the traditional caretaking role. In our case, we studied gay fathers (Benson, Silverstein, & Auerbach, 2002).

Central or Critical Case Sampling

The strategy of central or critical case sampling involves choosing a research sample in which you assume that your theoretical construct will be present, and of central importance to the sample. This is called critical case sampling because if you find that the construct is not present or important to the sample under study, you will have to revise your basic assumptions.

With reference to the construct, RELIGIOUS FACILITATING IDEOLOGY, possible central or critical case samples are Orthodox Jewish fathers and Promise Keeper fathers, because we assume that religion is central to these fathers' lives. We studied both of these groups (Backer-Bolensky, 1998; Paragon, 1998; Silverstein, Auerbach, Grieco, & Dunkel, 1999).

Typical or Paradigm Case Sampling

The strategy of typical or paradigm case sampling involves choosing a research sample whose situation is typical or common in everyday life, so that you can see how your theoretical constructs operate in ordinary experience. Your research results can then serve as examples or paradigms for making your theoretical constructs real and tangible to research consumers.

Possible examples of this strategy are fathers in dual-career couples, and stepfathers. These family forms are common in people's ordinary experience, so that studying role strain in these contexts would make the concept relevant to people's own lives. We have investigated fathers from both groups (Dunkel, Auerbach, & Silverstein, 2002; Weinberg, 1997).

Similar Case Sampling

The strategy of similar case sampling involves choosing several research samples whose relevant characteristics are similar but not identical to those of your original study. This allows you to investigate your theoretical constructs in situations resembling those you studied originally.

In the case of the Haitian Fathers Study, the relevant characteristic of the sample is that the fathers were immigrants. Possible similar case samples are other Haitian fathers and fathers from other immigrant groups. We used this strategy by investigating several different groups of Latino fathers (Peguero, Silversein, & Auerbach, 1999, 2000).

Sensitive or Political Case Sampling

The strategy of sensitive or political case sampling involves choosing a research sample from a group that is the subject of political debate, and hence is highly visible.

Possible examples of this strategy are young African American fathers, divorced fathers, and Promise Keeper fathers, each of whom are the subjects of much public discussion. We have studied each of these groups (Auerbach, Silverstein, & Zizi, 1997; Silverstein, Auerbach, Grieco, & Dunkel, 1999; Weil, 1997).

Our next research sample of Promise Keeper fathers illustrates several of these strategies simultaneously. They were a convenience sample for us because we had a graduate student who was herself a fundamentalist Christian and had access to this population. They were also a central case sample, because religion was a relevant part of their fathering experience. Finally, they were a political and sensitive case sample, because at the time of the study they were in the public eye.

Five Steps for Designing Your Next Study

Having described theoretical sampling in detail, we return to the steps in designing your next research study (see Table 9.3). We will describe these steps in more detail, and illustrate them with our research on Promise Keeper fathers.

Table 9.3 presents a five-step procedure for designing your next research study. If you examine the steps, you will see that you are already familiar with most of them, because they are similar to the five-step procedure for designing your *first* research study, which was given in chapter 2. However, thc sequence of steps is slightly different, because your next study grows out of your initial study rather than out of the research literature.

Table 9.3
A Five-Step Procedure for Designing Your Next Research Study or Sequence of Studies

1. State the research concerns and theoretical framework that have emerged from your first study.
2. Choose a research sample to investigate your research concerns and theoretical framework, using the strategies of theoretical sampling.
3. Review the research literature relevant to your new research sample in order to discover relevant background information, and also to elaborate your research concerns and theoretical framework.
4. Construct a narrative interview, based on the questions you retain from the previous study, and also on the new issues that have emerged from your literature review.
5. Continue this process until theoretical saturation is reached.

Step 1. State the Research Concerns and Theoretical Framework That Have Emerged from Your First Study

After you have completed your first study, your thinking about your research concerns will have changed considerably. You will be more familiar with the phenomenon, and will have developed your initial set of theoretical constructs. This first step asks you to make these changes in your thinking explicit, by stating your new research concerns and theoretical framework. You should find this step valuable because it will help you realize how far your research has come.

In our case, our initial research concerns were to explore men's subjective experience of fatherhood from a feminist and multicultural perspective. Upon completion of the Haitian Fathers Study, our thinking had become more focused. We had seen that the men were experiencing role strain as they tried to redefine fathering by integrating aspects of the more traditional (i.e., patriarchal) fathering role with behaviors associated with a more modern (i.e., egalitarian) fathering role. We were also interested in what role religion and religious ideology might play in facilitating the new role.

Thus, we formulated our new research concerns and theoretical framework in the following way.

1. To explore further how men were redefining the fathering role.
2. To elaborate the construct of role strain as it was experienced in the process of redefining the fathering role.

3. To obtain evidence for the constructs of facilitating ideology and social support.
4. To explore how religious ideas might provide a facilitating ideology for creating a more gratifying fathering role.

Step 2. Choose a Research Sample to Investigate Your Research Concerns and Theoretical Framework, Using the Strategies of Theoretical Sampling

After you have stated your research concerns and theoretical framework, the next step is to choose a research sample to investigate them further, using strategies for theoretical sampling. You should examine the list of strategies in Table 9.2 and select a strategy, or group of strategies, that meets your particular needs.

In our case, we chose the Promise Keepers for several reasons.

1. They were an organization that saw their mission as using religion to redefine fatherhood. Thus, in terms of our goal of exploring whether religious ideas could provide a facilitating ideology, they represented a central or critical case sample.
2. They were very much in the public eye and the topic of media attention. Therefore, they allowed us to use the strategy of sensitive or political case sample.
3. We had a fundamentalist Christian student who had access to the Promise Keepers, and therefore they were a convenience sample.

Step 3. Review the Research Literature Relevant to Your Research Sample to Discover Relevant Background Information and Further Elaborate Your Research Concerns and Theoretical Framework

After you have chosen a research sample, your next step is to learn more about it. For this purpose, a literature review is essential. The goal of this review is not to formulate hypotheses, but rather to clarify issues and to acquire information that may be relevant to your research concerns and theoretical framework.

In our case, we reviewed the literature on the Promise Keepers in the popular press and the academic literature. We learned that they were the subject of a controversy among progressives and feminists. On the one hand, their public statements that advocated restoring men's leadership within the traditional family seemed quite reactionary. On the other hand, they also proposed that men become more emotionally connected to their wives and their children. This perspective was consistent with feminist goals and seemed very progressive. When we did our research, therefore, we were sensitized to examining both the progressive the conservative elements in the Promise Keeper fathers.

Step 4. Construct a Narrative Interview, Based on the Issues and Topics That Have Emerged from Your Literature Review

As we have seen in chapter 2, the narrative interview is a major research instrument in designing your first qualitative research study. It remains central in designing subsequent studies.

In our case, the narrative interview repeated the questions of our Haitian Fathers Study, and added an additional question about how membership in the Promise Keepers affected the men's relationships with their wives and children. The research interviewer was instructed not to adhere to the specific questions too rigidly, but to follow up on issues that struck the research participants themselves as important. The questions we used are listed below.

1. What was the first time you thought about being a father, and what did you think it would be like?
2. What is your relationship with your father, and how has it affected your fathering?
3. How did you and your wife go through the process of deciding to have child?
4. What is being a father like? How did it change your sense of who you are, and what your life is about?
5. What are you most proud of, and what do you most regret?
6. How has being a father affected your relationship with your parents and siblings?
7. How has the Promise Keepers influenced your attitudes toward fathering?

It is worth noting that our research participants used these questions as a springboard to talk about issues that were important to them. The principle that the answers you get are more important than the questions you ask proved to be applicable here.

Step 5. Continue This Process until Theoretical Saturation Is Reached

When you complete and analyze your next study, you will probably find that it again leads you to reconsider your research concerns and theoretical framework. Step 5 instructs you to continue theoretical sampling until your research concerns are clear and your theoretical framework no longer changes.

We call this point theoretical saturation, which brings us to the issue of determining sample size in qualitative research studies. We have already discussed theoretical sampling in chapter 2, and we will elaborate that material here.

With random sampling, in which the goal is to achieve a representative sample, the statistical technique of power analysis is used to determine the sample size necessary to produce a representative sample. With theoretical sampling, in contrast, in which the goal is to extend and refine your theoretical constructs, sample size is determined by the method of *theoretical saturation*. Here is how it works. After your first study, each new research sample will refine your theoretical constructs, and give you new information and new insights. After you have completed several studies with new samples, however, you will find that additional research samples do not add any new information to your understanding of your theoretical constructs. Rather, additional studies simply confirm what you already know. At this point you do not need to do any more sampling. You have reached theoretical saturation.

> Theoretical saturation is the research sampling strategy in which you continue to study new research samples until you are simply confirming the theory that you have already developed, rather than modifying or elaborating it.

Here is how theoretical saturation applies to the role strain construct. In the Yeshiva Fatherhood Project we studied fathers from many different subcultures. We found that fathers in all of our samples were experiencing some form of role strain. It is worth noting, however, that in each subculture we studied, role strain took a different, culturally specific form.

Describing the Promise Keeper Fathers

We will close this chapter by describing our research sample of Promise Keeper fathers. Promise Keepers is an evangelical Christian organization founded by the former head football coach of the University of Colorado, Bill McCartney. His view, based on his own experience as a husband and a father, was that men had focused too much on their work lives. As a result, they have not kept their marital promise to be responsible to their wives and their families. The goal of his movement is to get the men to keep the promises they made upon marriage; hence the name, Promise Keepers.

The Promise Keeper sample consisted of a group of 22 men ranging in age from their late twenties to their early sixties. Two of the men were African American, and the other 20 were white and Euro-American. The men all came from New Jersey and were predominantly middle class. They had between one and four children. For a more detailed description of the research sample, consult the research article, provided in Appendix C.

10

■ ■ ■ ■ ■ ■ ■ ■ ■

Analyzing Your Next Study Using Elaborative Coding

The Promise Keeper Fathers

THE PREVIOUS CHAPTER EXPLAINED how to design your next study. This chapter will discuss how to analyze it. Herein we describe a procedure for analyzing data to develop your theory further, and illustrate the procedure with material from our research on Promise Keeper fathers.

Six Steps for Elaborative Coding

The procedure for analyzing the data from your next study is called *elaborative coding.*

> Elaborative coding is the process of analyzing textual data in order to develop theory further.

Elaborative coding is called "top-down" coding because one begins coding with the theoretical constructs from the previous study in mind. This contrasts with the coding one does in an initial study (bottom-up), where relevant text is selected without preconceived ideas in mind. In elaborative coding where the goal is to refine theoretical constructs from a previous study, relevant text is selected with those constructs in mind.

Table 10.1

Six Steps for Elaborative Coding Aimed at Refining Old Constructs, Developing New Ones, and Constructing a Theoretical Narrative from Text

MAKING THE TEXT MANAGEABLE

1. Explicitly state your new research concerns, your theoretical constructs, and what you want to develop further.
2. Select the relevant text for further analysis. Do this by reading through the raw text with Step 1 in mind, highlighting relevant text. Select text that is consistent with your old theoretical constructs, as well as text that suggests new ones.

HEARING WHAT WAS SAID

3. Record repeating ideas by grouping together related passages of relevant text. Organize the repeating ideas with respect to old and potentially new theoretical constructs.
4. Organize themes by grouping repeating ideas into coherent categories. As before, the organization of themes should reflect old and potentially new theoretical constructs.

DEVELOPING THEORY

5. Elaborate old theoretical constructs by grouping themes into units consistent with them. Develop any new theoretical constructs by organizing themes into meaningful units.
6. Create a theoretical narrative by retelling the participants' story in terms of both old and new theoretical constructs.

The Promise Keeper Study provides an example of elaborative coding. We collected interview data from Promise Keeper fathers in order to develop further the theoretical constructs of BICULTURAL GENDER ROLE STRAIN, CONSTRUCTING A MORE GRATIFYING DEFINITION OF FATHERHOOD, RELIGIOUS FACILITATING IDEOLOGY, and SOCIAL SUPPORT.

As you will see, we found support for the theoretical construct of role strain. For the Promise Keeper fathers, role strain was experienced because traditional gender role norms failed to bring them the happiness they expected. We also found support for the two theoretical constructs of FACILITATING IDEOLOGY and SOCIAL SUPPORTS. However, we were led to revise the theoretical construct of CONSTRUCTING A MORE GRATIFYING DEFINITION OF FATHERHOOD. As we came to understand what the fathers were telling us in a more nuanced way, we changed this construct to PERSONAL GRATIFICATION: CONNECTING TO GOD AND FAMILY. Our theoretical constructs for the Promise Keeper fathers are given in Table C.3 of the original article, which we will explain in this chapter.

Table 10.1 presents a six-step procedure for doing elaborative coding of the data from your next research study. The step are slightly different from the six steps for coding data from your *first* research study given in chapters 5, 6, and 7, because you already have the theoretical constructs from your first study to work with. Therefore, you do not have to develop theoretical constructs from scratch. As before, even though we present the steps linearly, the coding process involves a nonlinear back and forth movement between later steps and earlier ones.

In what follows, we will explain the six steps in detail, and work through their application to the Promise Keepers Study. Although new studies can yield new theoretical constructs as well as elaborate and refine previous constructs, our presentation will cover only the procedure for elaborating old constructs, since the procedure for discovering new constructs was already described in chapters 5, 6, and 7.

Making the Text Manageable

Step 1. Explicitly State Your New Research Concerns and Theoretical Framework, Your Theoretical Constructs, and What You Want to Develop Further

As with the original coding procedure, the first step will force you to focus on the goal of your data analysis. As before, you should begin by stating the research concerns that resulted from your first study. In particular, you should reflect on how your theoretical framework has changed in response to your earlier research. Be as explicit as you can about your new theoretical framework. Finally, you should enumerate the theoretical constructs you want to develop further. You will have already done this work when you thought about choosing your research sample, discussed in chapter 9, so that you can just remind yourself of your earlier work.

When we began to analyze the Promise Keeper data, we had already developed our four basic theoretical constructs. We had seen that men's subjective experience of fatherhood involved redefining the fathering role in response to role strain associated with the traditional role. We also wanted to know how religion and religious facilitating ideology helped to create a new role. Thus we formulated our new research concerns, theoretical framework, and constructs that we wanted to develop in the following way.

1. To further explore how men were redefining the fathering role.
2. To elaborate the constructs of role strain and redefining the fathering role, and to obtain evidence for the constructs of facilitating ideology and social support.
3. To explore how religion can serve as a facilitating ideology for creating a more gratifying fathering role.

Step 2. Select the Relevant Text for Further Analysis, by Reading Through the Raw Text with Step 1 in Mind, Highlighting Relevant Text. Select Text That Is Consistent with Your Old Theoretical Constructs, as Well as Text That Suggests New Ones

Once again, start reading through the transcripts. As you read, keep in mind both your new research concerns and the old theoretical constructs that you want to develop further. Whenever you encounter a passage of text that is relevant to your research concerns, your theoretical constructs, or both, highlight that passage. Each of the passages that you select is *relevant text*, that is, text relevant to your research concerns.

It is now important to keep a memo of your thoughts while you are doing the highlighting. (When you analyzed the data from your first study, keeping a memo was optional.) At a minimum, the memo should record the theoretical construct, if any, with which the highlighted text fits. In addition, you may want to record why you find the text relevant and any other thoughts suggested by the text.

Sometimes the relevant text that you select will fit with your old theoretical constructs. This is helpful because it will lead you to develop your constructs further. On other occasions, however, the relevant text will not fit with one of your old theoretical constructs, but instead will suggest new ones. This is also helpful, because it will increase your understanding of your research concerns.

Continue this process until you have read through all of the transcripts. As before, deciding what is relevant is up to you, and you will develop your own criteria as you go along. When you are done, copy the relevant text into separate files, one for each focus group (or for each individual if you are doing individual interviews).

The process can be illustrated with an example from the Promise Keeper

Table 10.2

Transcript and Underlined Relevant Text for the Promise Keeper Data

J2: For me, it's nice to not do all the talking. My wife says I dominate sometimes, but . . . For me it's very easy. [I do the opposite of what my dad did, and I try to figure that must be right.] Again, it's tough to talk about parents. I respect my folks for doing the best job they knew how. As parents, they were saying, [you go to adopt, they have to almost train you or test you to make sure you're qualified. And we've joked about it, as parents there should be a test. There should be a licensing procedure.] And so I have, I think the Lord has given me a discerning ability and a sensitive nature to know that my father was not one that would harm anyone intentionally. But again, only did as much as he was taught. So I had more sympathy for his inability to share his feelings in an open way as I have tried to incorporate with my wife and children. Our relationship on the surface is excellent. You know he's still around. He had a heart condition and he's still healthy. We share a lot of time together. We're in the same town and I've had the opportunity to share my faith and so everything that I'm about revolves around my faith. And he needs to, I need to understand where he's coming from, but he needs to know that, you know, this is who I am and so we learn from each another. I still learn a lot of things from him. [But on the sensitive side, I don't think I learned anything from him] and I'm just blessed that the Lord has given me that ability to want to share with my wife and doing a so-so job with the kids. We have, you know, the hugging and this and that. But I think I have a different expectation of each. My son, I expect him to be a little tougher and to have a little more ability to bounce back and be strong. My daughters are much more sensitive.

Source: Grieco. 1996, pp. 194–196.

fathers, involving the theoretical construct of role strain. The raw text that we will consider is shown in Table 10.2, which also shows how we highlighted the text to indicate passages relevant to role strain. The speaker, J2, is responding to the moderator's earlier question concerning the men's relationship with their own fathers.

The first relevant text, RT#1, reads:

I do the opposite of what my dad did, and I try to figure that must be right. (J2, p. 194)

Our memo for RT#1 is:

ROLE STRAIN
Father as a negative role model

Our memo indicates that RT#1 fits with our theoretical construct of role strain. It states that J2 has a problem with the traditional fathering role, as his father performed it. The memo also paraphrases the idea in the relevant text that the father is a negative role model, that he is an example of how not to be a father.

RT#2 and its memo read:

> you go to adopt, they have to almost train you or test you to make sure you're qualified. And we've joked about it, as parents there should be a test. There should be a licensing procedure. (J2, p. 194)
>
> ROLE STRAIN
>
> Difficulty in parenting creates a need for a definite procedure.

Our memo indicates that RT#2 fits in with our theoretical construct of role strain, expressing the idea that the parenting role is so difficult that not everyone should be a parent.

RT#3 and its memo read:

> But on the sensitive side, I don't think I learned anything from him. (J2, p. 195)
>
> ROLE STRAIN
>
> Father does not provide a model for parenting that is sensitive to the child.

The idea expressed in RT#3 is related to the idea expressed in RT#1; in RT#1, J2 says that his father was a negative role model, and in RT#3 he states that his father was not a role model at all.

After you have selected all the relevant text, make a file for it and save the file in your larger project folder. Create a separate file for each group. As before, maintaining careful and detailed records is very important. And, as before, each page should have a header that includes the project, the group, the date the coding was completed, and the name of the coder.

Hearing What Was Said

Step 3. Record Repeating Ideas by Grouping Together Related Passages of Relevant Text. Organize the Repeating Ideas with Respect to Old and Potentially New Theoretical Constructs

At this point, the procedure is almost identical to the one in chapter 6, the only difference being that here you use your theoretical constructs in developing the repeating ideas. You are already familiar with the process of creating repeating ideas, so we will present the procedure in an abbreviated form, given in Table 10.3.

We will illustrate this procedure with the small list of relevant text shown in Table 10.4.

Table 10.3

Step 3. The Procedure for Using Theoretical Constructs to Create Repeating Ideas from Relevant Text

1. Begin by creating a list of repeating ideas for group 1.
   a. Open the file that contains the list of relevant text for group 1, which we call the working list of group 1 relevant text.
   b. Group these ideas under the theoretical construct that you assigned to them in your memo. If you did not assign them a theoretical construct, leave them ungrouped. You will code the ideas associated with each theoretical construct separately.
   c. For each theoretical construct, create a list of repeating ideas for the relevant text associated with it.
      i. Begin with the starter text (see chapter 6) for the first repeating idea. Read through your working list of relevant text and select all text similar to the starter text and therefore to each other. The text you have selected is the relevant text for the first repeating idea.
      ii. Remove the text selected above, and analyze the remaining text in the same way.
      iii. Continue this process until all the relevant text for group 1 is analyzed into repeating ideas.
      iv. Deal with orphans, ideas too broad, and ideas too narrow, in the same way that you did in chapter 6.
2. Repeat the process above for your remaining groups.
3. Combine the repeating ideas for each group into a master list of repeating ideas for all the groups. Do this the same way that you did in chapter 6.
4. Name your repeating ideas by assigning to each a quote or paraphrase that captures their essence in a dramatic and emotionally vivid way.
5. Check your organization of the data with that of your co-researchers. The procedure here is the same as that in chapter 6.

Table 10.4

A Sample of a Master List of Relevant Text from the Promise Keeper Father Research

(a) I do the opposite of what my dad did, and I try to figure that must be right (J2, p. 194)

ROLE STRAIN

Father as a negative role model.

(b) you go to adopt, they have to almost train you or test you to make sure you're qualified. And we've joked about it, as parents there should be a test. There should be a licensing procedure. (J2, p. 194)

ROLE STRAIN

Difficulty in parenting creates a need for a definite procedure.

(c) But on the sensitive side, I don't think I learned anything from him. (J2, p. 195)

ROLE STRAIN

Father does not provide a model for parenting that is sensitive to the child.

(d) I recall just two nights ago my son was bending over to tie the dog down and he hit his head on the countertop. And he tends to be very dramatic. I told him he's going to be an actor, a politician. But I did not have an open, loving response. It was more, you're okay and I don't see any blood and it's just about learning everyday. I need to be sensitive to him. How else will he learn what it is to be sensitive to others, to his wife, to his children? (J2, p. 195)

ROLE STRAIN

Recognition of his own problems as a parent in not being sensitive enough to his son.

(e) I was for the most part a woman's man in the negative sense in that I was raised by my mother. I didn't have my father and I noticed even in dialogues with my wife, that's something a woman would do, something a man would do. (J1, p. 79)

ROLE STRAIN

Absence of father leaves him uncertain about manhood.

(f) So it was very different. I had to find images. I had to find, pick and choose, almost like picking out a meal, I had to find those glimmers of manhood, and strive to understand what manhood was. (J1, p. 80)

ROLE STRAIN

Absence of father forces him to create his own model.

(g) And in the early days, I was thinking, there was no manual. There's no document that says, okay, you're going to get married, here's the book on what you need to do to be a good husband, what you need to do to be a good father, what is a good father. (J1, p. 80)

ROLE STRAIN

Absence of a father leads to uncertainty about how to be a father.

(h) During my teenage years we really had a stormy relationship and I think unless it had been for my faith, I wouldn't have gotten through that in a healthy way. (F, p. 80)

ROLE STRAIN

A bad relationship with father.

(continued)

Table 10.4 *(continued)*

(i) Until I got to be a teenager I didn't see much of my father. He'd be gone in the morning to work before I got up and the majority of times I would be in bed before he came home from work. (J3, p. 80)

ROLE STRAIN

A distant relationship with father, due to father occupying only the traditional provider role.

(j) But this made me realize when I had my children to try and spend as much time with them as possible. If the group from church was going on a camping trip or something, try to get in on the camping trip with them because they really enjoy it when you go along. (J3, p. 80)

ROLE STRAIN

Defining being a father as doing the opposite of what own father does.

We begin with the starter text under ROLE STRAIN, labeled (a), which together with its memo is:

(a) I do the opposite of what my dad did, and I try to figure that must be right. (J2, p. 194)

Father as a negative role model.

We read through the remaining working list of relevant text until we encounter text expressing ideas similar to (a). Before you read further, try this yourself and compare your choices with the ones we made.

In this case the items of relevant text are (c) and (j), which, together with their memos, read:

(c) But on the sensitive side, I don't think I learned anything from him. (J2, p. 195)

Father does not provide a model for parenting that is sensitive to the child.

(j) But this made me realize when I had my children to try and spend as much time with them as possible. If the group from church was going on a camping trip or something, try to get in on the camping trip with them because they really enjoy it when you go along. (J3, p. 80)

Defining being a father as doing the opposite of what own father does.

What relevant text (a), (c), and (j) have in common is their concern with the father as a role model. Text (a) talks about the father as a negative role model; text (c) talks about the father not being a role model at all; and text (j) talks about being a father by spending time with one's children in a way one's own father did not. This common concern will later figure in naming the first idea.

Having selected relevant text for the first repeating idea, the remaining items of relevant text are (b), (d), (e), (f), (g), and (i).

The first relevant text, (b), is the starter text for the second repeating idea.

Text (b), together with its memo, reads:

> (b) you go to adopt, they have to almost train you or test you to make sure you're qualified. And we've joked about it, as parents there should be a test. There should be a licensing procedure. (J2, p. 194)
>
> Difficulty in parenting creates a need for a definite procedure.

We then read through the rest of the reduced list until we encountered repeating ideas similar to (b). Before you read further, try this yourself and compare your choices with ours.

The first relevant text we encounter is (e) which, together with its memo, reads:

> (e) I was for the most part a woman's man in the negative sense in that I was raised by my mother. I didn't have my father and I noticed even in dialogues with my wife, that's something a woman would do, something a man would do. (J1, p. 79)
>
> Absence of father leaves him uncertain about manhood.

Both (b) and (e) express the idea of uncertainty about what is involved in being a father.

Reading further, we encounter the relevant text (f) and (g), which also express the idea of uncertainty about what is involved in being a father. These relevant texts, together with their memos, read:

> (f) So it was very different. I had to find images. I had to find, pick and choose, almost like picking out a meal, I had to find those glimmers of manhood, and strive to understand what manhood was. (J1, p. 80)
>
> Absence of father forces him to create his own model.

(g) And in the early days, I was thinking, there was no manual. There's no document that says, okay, you're going to get married, here's the book on what you need to do to be a good husband, what you need to do to be a good father, what is a good father. (J1, p. 80)

Absence of a father leads to uncertainty about how to be a father.

At this point, then, we have gathered the relevant text for the second repeating idea.

Our new reduced list consists of relevant text (h) and (i). When we read through this reduced list we can find no more repeating ideas.

Now we must name the repeating ideas with a vivid phrase that captures their essence. The relevant text for naming the first repeating idea is:

(a) I do the opposite of what my dad did, and I try to figure that must be right. (J2, p. 194)

Father as a negative role model

(c) But on the sensitive side, I don't think I learned anything from him. (J2, p. 195)

Father does not provide a model for parenting that is sensitive to the child.

(j) But this made me realize when I had my children to try and spend as much time with them as possible. If the group from church was going on a camping trip or something, try to get in on the camping trip with them because they really enjoy it when you go along. (J3, p. 80)

Defining being a father as doing the opposite of what own father does.

Reading through this text in search of vivid language, we are struck by the language in (a): "I do the opposite of what my dad did, and I figure that must be right." We could have used this to name the first repeating idea. However, after we had read through the all of the transcripts, we found "I know how not to be a father," which was the name we used.

The relevant text for naming the second repeating idea is:

(b) you go to adopt, they have to almost train you or test you to make sure you're qualified. And we've joked about it, as parents there should be a test. There should be a licensing procedure. (J2, p. 194)

Difficulty in parenting creates a need for a definite procedure.

(e) I was for the most part a woman's man in the negative sense in that I was raised by my mother. I didn't have my father and I noticed even in dialogues with my wife, that's something a woman would do, something a man would do. (J1, p. 79)

Absence of father leaves him uncertain about manhood.

(f) So it was very different. I had to find images. I had to find, pick and choose, almost like picking out a meal, I had to find those glimmers of manhood, and strive to understand what manhood was. (J1, p. 80)

Absence of father forces him to create his own model.

(g) And in the early days, I was thinking, there was no manual. There's no document that says, okay, you're going to get married, here's the book on what you need to do to be a good husband, what you need to do to be a good father, what is a good father. (J1, p. 80)

Absence of a father leads to uncertainty about how to be a father.

Reading through this text in search of vivid language we are struck by the language in (b) "I had to find images," and in (g) "There was no manual," either of which could have named the second repeating idea. However, after we had read through the all of the transcripts, we found the phrase "Feeling unprepared to be a father," which was what we used.

Step 4. Organize Themes by Grouping Repeating Ideas into Coherent Categories. As Before, the Organization of Themes Should Reflect Old and Potentially New Theoretical Constructs

As was the case with Step 3, the procedure in Step 4 is almost identical to the one in chapter 6, the only difference being that your repeating ideas are already grouped into theoretical constructs. You are already familiar with the process for creating themes, so we will present the procedure in an abbreviated form, given in Table 10.5.

As an illustration of how to create themes from repeating ideas, consider the small list of seven repeating ideas presented below. They are taken from Table C.3 of the Promise Keepers paper, and are the seven repeating ideas associated with role strain, but given in a scrambled order. In several cases

Table 10.5

Step 4. The Procedure for Using Theoretical Constructs to Create Themes from Repeating Ideas

1. Open your list of repeating ideas, which are now organized according to your theoretical constructs.
2. Begin with your first theoretical construct and create a working list of repeating ideas for that construct.
   a. Begin with the starter idea (see chapter 6) for the first theme. Read through your working list of repeating ideas and select all the ideas similar to the starter idea, and therefore to each other. The text you have selected is the relevant text for the first theme.
   b. Remove the text selected above and analyze the remaining text the same way to get your second theme.
   c. Continue this process until all the repeating ideas for your first theoretical construct are analyzed into themes.
   d. Deal with orphans, ideas too broad, and ideas too narrow in the same way you did in chapter 6.
3. Repeat the process for your remaining theoretical constructs.
4. Name your themes with an easily understood phrase that expresses what they have in common.
5. Discuss your themes with a consultant who is a member of the culture of your research sample, or very familiar with it, and make whatever changes emerge from that discussion.

we have slightly changed the wording of the Promise Keepers paper, in such a way as to make the names more vivid and descriptive.

(a) "I realized that I wasn't prepared to be a father."
(b) "I built a wall up and isolated myself."
(c) "I know how not to be a father."
(d) "A man has to be strong."
(e) "My father was never really around."
(f) "I got kind of scared about being a father."
(g) "Providing is everything."

We developed the first theme by focusing our attention on repeating idea (a) "I realized that I wasn't prepared to be a father," and reading down the repeating idea list until we encountered an idea similar to (a). Before you read further, do this yourself and compare your choice with ours.

We read down the list until we encountered repeating idea (f) "I got kind of scared about being a father." Repeating ideas (a) and (f) are similar in that both express the common theme of uncertainty about fatherhood. We found no more repeating ideas similar to (a). Therefore, (a) and (f) are the repeating ideas for the first role strain theme.

The remaining text, formed by deleting (a) and (f) from the original list, is

(b) "I built a wall up and isolated myself."
(c) "I know how not to be a father."
(d) "A man has to be strong."
(e) "My father was never really around."
(g) "Providing is everything."

We developed the second theme by focusing on repeating idea (b) "I built a wall up and isolated myself," and reading down the reduced list until we found repeating ideas similar to (b). Again, try it yourself before reading further.

The ideas similar to (b) were (d) "A man has to be strong," and (g) "Providing is everything," each of which expressed the common theme of traditional masculinity. This group of repeating ideas defined our second role strain theme.

Finally, we were left with the remaining text:

(c) "I know how not to be a father."
(e) "My father was never really around."

Both these ideas expressed the common theme of unhappiness with their own fathers, and so constituted our third role strain theme.

Having grouped the repeating ideas into themes, we named the themes with a phrase that expressed what the repeating ideas had in common. As you can see in Table C.3 of the article, we named the themes *Unhappy early experiences with their fathers* [repeating ideas (c) and (e)], *Struggling with their own fathering* [repeating ideas (a) and (f)], and *Relying on the traditional masculine role* [repeating ideas (b), (d), and (g)].

Developing Theory

Step 5. Elaborate Old Theoretical Constructs by Showing How Themes Are Consistent with Them

In Step 5, you begin to develop theory. The procedure for developing theory is somewhat different from the one in chapter 7, where developing theory meant starting with the themes you have and then organizing them into theoretical constructs. In this chapter, however, you start with both the themes and the theoretical constructs. In fact, the themes were created with the theoretical constructs in mind. So, rather than developing theoretical constructs from scratch, you use your themes to elaborate the constructs that you already have. Table 10.6 describes a procedure for doing this.

The goal of the procedure is to discover the *specific* form your theoretical constructs take when applied to your *current* research sample. With the Promise Keepers, for example, you will discover the specific form that gender role strain takes for Promise Keeper fathers. After analyzing your data you will understand more about your theoretical constructs, your themes, and how they relate to each other.

Although we present the procedure as a series of sequential tasks, this is only for purposes of exposition. Like everything else in qualitative research, the procedure is nonlinear. It is a back and forth process, in which the results of the later tasks will lead you to go back and revise the earlier ones.

We will illustrate the procedure of Step 5 by showing how the themes developed in Step 4 improved our understanding of the gender role strain construct. As you read further, you will probably notice that our current analysis considerably expands upon the theory presented in the Promise Keepers paper. Since studying the Promise Keepers, we have studied many more samples of fathers, and so have elaborated on the theory.

If you need to remind yourself of the themes, take another look at Table C.3 (in Appendix C) before you read further.

For the first task in Table 10.6, we focus our thinking by reminding ourselves of the exact meaning of gender role strain, our theoretical construct. Gender role strain refers to the conflicts and tensions created by a gender role, by the male gender role in particular. Fatherhood, of course, is part of the male gender role. When we examine our themes, therefore, we will

Table 10.6

Step 5. The Procedure for Integrating Your Theoretical Constructs with Your Themes to Increase Your Understanding of Both

1. Remind yourself, as explicitly and directly as you can, of the definition and meaning of the theoretical construct that you want to elaborate.
2. Examine your themes and state as explicitly as you can how they fit together with the theoretical construct and with each other. Do this until you can make a clear and coherent statement. In the process you may find yourself reconceptualizing both your theoretical construct and your themes.
3. Name your theoretical construct for your research sample. The name should specify the *specific form* your theoretical construct takes for this particular research sample. It should reflect the understanding that you developed in Step 2, above.

focus on the ways they might exemplify the tensions and conflicts in the Promise Keepers' experience of masculinity and fatherhood.

Keeping the definition of gender role strain as our focus, we begin the second task, and examine the themes one by one. The first theme is *Unhappy early experience with their fathers,* which pertains to their fathers' physical and emotional absence and their father as a negative role model. We ask ourselves how these unhappy early experiences relate to conflicts and tensions about masculinity and fatherhood.

One of the ways that men learn about the fathering role is from the ways their own fathers behaved. If men are satisfied with how they were parented, they are able to emulate their fathers, and they should experience little or no role strain. On the other hand, if men are unhappy with how they were parented, they may experience a number of emotions that can generate role strain. For example, they may automatically behave like their father, even though they did not approve of his behavior. Alternatively, they may avoid acting like their father, but feel at a loss about how to behave. Uncertainty and internal conflict of this type produce gender role strain.

With this thought in mind, we turn to the second theme of *Struggling with their own fathering*, which addresses their anxiety about their own fathering, and feeling unprepared for fatherhood. We then ask ourselves how this theme relates to gender role strain. The answer is clear. Some of the men felt at a loss about how to act as parents. This uncertainty produced gender role strain.

We next turn to the third theme, trying to take our analysis further. The third theme, *Relying on the traditional masculine role*, reflects the fact that some of the men equated fatherhood with the stereotypic masculine ideals of being strong and being a good provider. The theme also describes how stereotypic masculinity creates a wall of emotional isolation. We again asked ourselves how this theme connects with gender role strain.

The men dealt with their uncertainties about how to be a father by trying to live up to the traditional masculine stereotype. However, their extreme focus on providing financial security caused them to be away from home so much that they missed many important events in their children's lives. Similarly, their focus on being strong made it difficult for them to be emotionally intimate with their children. Thus, although they were conforming to the behavior expected from "a good father," they felt emotionally isolated from their children, and left out of family life in general. Consequently, they were doing what they were supposed to be doing, according to traditional masculinity ideology, but it was not bringing them happiness. This paradox increased their role strain further.

We may summarize our thinking so far as follows. Many of the men had unhappy experiences with their own fathers (theme 1). They felt uncertain about how to be a father (theme 2). In the absence of a good working model of how to be a parent, they relied on traditional stereotypes of how to be a father (theme 3). These stereotypes left them feeling emotionally isolated and left out of family life. In this way, the Promise Keeper fathers were experiencing gender role strain associated with the fathering role.

Notice what this analysis accomplishes: It describes the specific form that gender role strain takes for the Promise Keeper fathers, and it does so in terms of the themes. As a result, we understand more about gender role strain, our themes, and their interconnections.

Our final task is to name the specific form of role strain that we discovered, choosing a name that reflects our thinking up to this point. The name we chose was GENDER ROLE STRAIN: FAILURE OF TRADITIONAL MASCULINE NORMS. The expression captures the idea that enacting the traditional role norms did not bring the fathers happiness. They did not feel good about themselves as parents, nor did they feel emotionally connected to their children.

We named the other constructs in the same way. You can refer to the original paper for the details.

Step 6: Create a Theoretical Narrative by Retelling the Participants' Stories in Terms of Your Theoretical Constructs

The final step pulls everything together into a theoretical narrative that retells the participants' story in the language of your theoretical constructs. The procedure for constructing a theoretical narrative is the same as the one in chapter 6.

We conclude our discussion of elaborative coding by presenting a theoretical narrative summarizing our work with the Promise Keeper fathers.

> Our research participants joined the Promise Keepers because they were unhappy with their performance as husbands and fathers, and hoped that membership in the Promise Keepers would help them be more successful. Here is the story of how that happened.
>
> The decision to join the Promise Keepers was motivated by participants' dissatisfaction with the traditional fathering role to which they had been exposed (GENDER ROLE STRAINS: FAILURE OF TRADITIONAL GENDER ROLE NORMS). Their dissatisfaction had several aspects. They did not learn to be a father from their own fathers (*Unhappy early experience with their own fathers*). Often "he was never really around," and when he was present he only served as an example of "how not to be a father." As a result of these unhappy early experiences, the men did not know how to be fathers themselves (*Struggling with their own fathering*). They were "scared about being a father" and felt "unprepared to be a father." They coped as best they could by trying to make themselves into the traditional image of a father (*Relying on the traditional male role*), in which "a man has to be strong" because "providing is everything." As a result, they "built a wall around themselves," becoming "isolated from their wives and children."
>
> Motivated by these dissatisfactions, they searched for a new way of being a father and reconnecting with their family (FACILITATING IDEOLOGY: A NEW HUSBAND/FATHER PARADIGM). Promise Keepers met their needs. It taught them to value family life more than material success (*Your family is the most important part of your life*). They learned that "relations are the most important thing" and that listening is an "alternative to anger" in maintaining relationships. Promise Keepers helped them occupy the leadership position that men should have in families ("Men must accept the leadership role"). This involved recognizing that they were "the spiritual leaders of their

families." However, leadership was not tyranny; they learned that "you can only lead by serving," and that "men and women are different but equal."

Promise keepers taught them that they couldn't get through life or fatherhood alone (SOCIAL SUPPORTS: A BROTHERHOOD OF MEN). It was a source of ***male support***, so that "they weren't alone," and "could acknowledge their vulnerabilities."

Belonging to Promise Keepers helped them change their lives for the better (PERSONAL GRATIFICATION: CONNECTING TO GOD AND TO FAMILY). They learned that being a family man was *Doing God's work*, because "your family is a gift from god." They also ***reconnected with their family***, from whom they had been isolated, "improving their relationship with their wife" and also "improving their relationship with their extended family."

FINAL THOUGHTS

Part V

11

The "Why" of Qualitative Research

A Personal View

UNTIL THIS POINT IN THE BOOK, we have focused on the mechanics of qualitative research, what one might call the "how" of qualitative research. But now, at the conclusion of the book, we want to broaden our perspective and present our own view about why it is important to do qualitative research, and where our own research is going.

One of the critical questions that researchers struggle with is: Are there any ways of doing research so that the findings can only be used for good purposes? Specifically, we asked ourselves: How can our work benefit the nondominant and marginalized groups in society?

A good friend of Louise's, Sue Zalk, warned us when we began our research on fathers that, although we were coming to this research with feminist goals in mind, all research can potentially be used against women. Unfortunately, Sue's warning has proven to be true. As we have been catapulted into the "fatherhood wars," we have come to think more carefully about the ways in which research can be used.

Our goal has always been to *change* the world, not simply to *describe* it. So we have been left with our question: "How can we be of use in the struggle for social justice?" Although quantitative research can also be used to benefit marginalized groups, there are certain characteristics of qualitative research that we believe make it particularly appropriate for

Table 11.1

Characteristics of the Qualitative Paradigm That Contribute to Power Sharing

1. The qualitative paradigm focuses on the voices of the participants. Therefore, the experts are the participants, rather than the researchers.
2. The research is hypothesis-generating, rather than hypothesis-testing. This acknowledges that:
   a. There are variations in experience, rather than a universal norm.
   b. The researcher may not know enough about the phenomenon under study to generate a valid hypothesis.
3. There is an assumption of collaboration and partnership between the researcher and the participants. This makes it more likely that the outcome of the research may be relevant to improving the lives of the participants, and not simply furthering the career of the researcher.
4. The qualitative paradigm includes a reflexive stance that provides the opportunity for the researcher to examine her or his biases. Accepting the responsibility for examining oneself increases the probability that the research process will not be exploitative or oppressive for the participants.

contributing to a social action agenda. These characteristics are summarized in Table 11.1.

We have mentioned much of this in passing throughout the book, but now we will focus on these aspects of the qualitative paradigm. All of these points contribute to decreasing the power imbalance between researcher and participants.

Our use of the qualitative paradigm has been to *start with* the study of nondominant groups, and then *move to* the study of dominant groups. This sequence of research establishes two important principles:

a. The experiences of nondominant populations are just as important and worthy of study as those of the dominant population.
b. Nondominant groups can contribute knowledge that is relevant to the dominant group as well. These two ideas make a small contribution toward shifting the balance of power in society by bringing marginalized groups from the margin to the center of scientific discourse.

In our own work, we have tried to accomplish these goals in a variety of ways. First, we have embedded the concept of difference into the foundation of our research questions. For example, when we began our large-scale project on fathering, we did not ask, "How do fathers (in the abstract) experience parenting?" Rather, we asked, "How do different subcultures of fathers experience parenting?"

Given our membership in the white middle class, we are always at risk for assuming that our experience is the human experience. If we had stated our research question in the abstract, we might have been tempted to imagine that there was one, more or less universal, fathering experience. Thus, from the beginning, we reminded ourselves that different subcultures would have different experiences of the fathering role. The qualitative paradigm was helpful in this quest to avoid universalizing, because it does not assume that any single sample can be "representative" of the human experience.

Another goal of our work has been to counter the "official story" by highlighting silenced voices or marginalized voices. For example, we have recently completed two research projects on young, mostly unmarried, parents. These two studies have shown how some young fathers and young mothers are leading responsible and rich lives, even in the context of early, unmarried child bearing (Edwards & Silverstein, 2003; Solash & Silverstein, 2000).

The point of this work has been to provide positive portraits of these young people in order to counter the uniformly negative stereotypes that have defined the scientific and political discourse about "teen pregnancy" and "the promiscuous young black male." We are currently beginning a project on "children of divorce" who are in positive intimate relationships, in contrast to the official story that these adult children inevitably have relationship problems.

The qualitative paradigm allowed us to hear these silenced voices, because we did not have to develop a hypothesis going into the study. The stories of our participants contrasted so dramatically with the "official" story about them, that we could not have developed a relevant hypothesis. Thus, we could not have imagined that the 20 young mothers we studied were able to go to school, work, and take care of their toddlers simultaneously. Our hypothesis would most likely have focused on stress and failure, whereas their lives exuded resilience and success. The qualitative paradigm allowed us to enter the research with the simple goal of hearing their stories—hence enabling us to do so.

A more recent goal that emerged during the research process has been to show how research about nondominant groups, such as immigrant Caribbean fathers and gay fathers, can contribute to knowledge about all fathers, including white, heterosexual, native-born fathers. Prior to the 1990s, most psychological research began with the experience of privileged groups as the normative standard. If the researcher studied other groups at all, these were measured against the normative standard, and difference was most often interpreted as deficit.

A more recent trend in the research community has been to begin with the study of nondominant groups, and then use knowledge gained in that context to understand something about more dominant groups. We began our research with Haitian fathers who happened to be members of a religious community in Brooklyn. These men described how their belief in Jesus as a warm and loving god helped them reconstruct their fathering identity. Modeling themselves on Jesus, they underplayed the stern and emotionally distant traditional Haitian fathering role, and added elements of the U.S. middle-class ideal of a nurturing father role.

This finding, about the importance of religious ideology in reconstructing a more emotionally connected fathering identity, was a totally unexpected finding for us. We then discovered, as we began to study a group of Promise Keeper fathers, that exactly the same phenomenon was occurring in this group of white, upper-middle class men from New Jersey.

The qualitative paradigm was helpful in this regard in an almost paradoxical way. Although it specifically rejects assumptions about universal phenomena and representative samples, the qualitative process has shown how findings from a very specific, nonrepresentative population can be applied to another very different sample population. Similarly, if we had begun with a hypothesis-testing stance, we almost certainly would have missed the importance of the men's identification with Jesus. Our secular bias would not have generated a hypothesis about the importance of religion in defining parenting in contemporary America.

We cannot take credit for embracing this new model of studying nondominant groups first. We stumbled upon it because our graduate students chose two religious groups as convenience samples early in our research project. The close temporal connection of studying these two groups of religious fathers allowed us to make the conceptual connections. However, we have recognized the importance of this approach, and we now assume that studying nondominant groups will contribute to knowledge about all groups. This new model for the construction of knowledge validates the experience of women, poor people, lesbigay individuals, and people of color moving these groups from the margins to the center of scientific discourse.

We have been least successful to date in establishing authentic collaborative relationships with our research participants. When we began our project, we built in a feedback session in which we shared our "findings," that is our interpretation of their stories, with our participants. We asked whether we had gotten their stories right. We often learned a great deal during these feedback sessions, and revised our interpretations of the text.

This part of the project design was a big shift for us. Our experience as traditional researchers was that one might consult with other scientists or colleagues in interpreting the results, but never with the participants. Within the traditional model, assuming that the "subjects" might correct the researcher was not routine. We felt very self-congratulatory about adding this phase to our research.

However, as we have continued on our journey of self-reflection, we realized that there is still much about the dominant discourse, or the discourse of domination, that we have not yet relinquished for ourselves. The self-reflexive component of the qualitative paradigm is particularly helpful on this point. We now are planning to adopt a model of "solidarity research," or participatory action research, in which the participants co-construct the research design.

The first phase in this new model would be for the participants to identify their most pressing research concerns. The participants would also choose the research methods. For example, in a study of effects on women of war-related violence reported recently by Mishler and Steinitz (2001), many of the women in their study could not read. So the research team created plays, stories, and folktales to help women who had been raped report their experiences. In a new study that we are undertaking to evaluate an experimental school for "troubled" youth, we are asking the teachers, parents, and students to collaborate with us in defining the research questions, choosing the methodology, and collecting the data. These kinds of complex, long-term projects require complex and long-term relationships with communities.

Even in the context of trusting relationships, it is unlikely that true action research will go smoothly. Ethical questions, such as what will be left in and what will be left out of the “findings,” who will interpret and disseminate the findings, and so on need to be continually negotiated. Researchers have the power to walk away from the problem, participants do not.

A commitment to this level of collaboration requires a fundamental change in the role of the researcher, if the goal of the research really does become the empowerment of the participants. Mishler and Steinitz have made the point that researchers interested in a social action agenda need to demonstrate that “we are standing with the participants, not simply speaking for them.” We often have introduced ourselves as “recovering traditional researchers.” We have only begun to realize that this snappy little quip covered how little recovery has actually taken place. As we embark on this adventure of more authentic collaboration, we hope that we will have the courage to change.

Appendix A

Simplifying the Bookkeeping with Qualitative Data Analysis Programs

The data analyses that you have learned to do by hand can also be done with a computer program called a qualitative data analysis program, or a QDA program for short. In this appendix we are going to explain how.

It is helpful to begin with a few general remarks about the use of computers in qualitative data analysis. When we introduce students to this topic, they often respond with "Great! Now I can just plug my transcripts into the program and it will do the analysis for me." Naturally, they expect to encounter difficulties in learning to use the program, but they assume that once they have mastered the program their data analysis problems will be solved.

This reaction is based on a serious misconception about how QDA programs work. Students think they are like statistical data analysis packages: You enter the data, specify the analysis you want done, enter a few keystrokes, and out pops your data analysis. Unfortunately, QDA programs do not work like this at all. Although such programs give you a set of tools for analyzing textual data, the tools neither apply themselves nor do your thinking for you. Only you can decide how you want to analyze your text;

once you've decide on an analysis, though, the QDA program can help you do it faster and more systematically.

We must warn you, however, that QDA programs are a mixed blessing. On the positive side, they extend the range of what you can do by hand. But on the negative side, they distance you from the text: You lose the total immersion that comes from analyzing your text by hand. Thus, deciding whether to analyze your data by computer or by hand is a real choice, and there is something to be said for either alternative. We suggest that you first learn to do the data analysis by hand, so that you can experience being fully in contact with your data. Only then will you be in a position to make an informed decision about whether to use a QDA program.

At present there are three major QDA programs on the market: NVIVO, Atlas.ti, and Ethnograph. You probably have heard of some or all of them. In addition, you may have heard of N5 and NUDIST, which are earlier versions of NVIVO. You can get more information about these programs by consulting their distributor, scolari publications, who have their own Website (scolari.com).

The average researcher cannot master all these programs, and so must decide which one to use. Our decision was to use NVIVO, the program that we will explain here. We decided to use NVIVO for two reasons. First, our coding methods translate naturally into NVIVO, as you will see. Second, most of the researchers with whom we have contact use NVIVO, and we wanted to be compatible with them. However, if you are already a user of Atlas.ti or ethnograph, we have spoken to experts who assure us that our analysis can be done with these programs as well.

We will begin by discussing how to do coding aimed at developing theory. This is the "bottom-up" coding described in chapters 5, 6, and 7. Then we'll discuss how to do coding aimed at elaborating theory, the "top-down" coding described in chapter 10.

In the material that follows, we assume that you already are familiar with the basics of NVIVO and simply need to know how to apply it to our form of data analysis. Consequently, our discussion will be somewhat abbreviated and schematic. If you want to learn more about NVIVO, we suggest that you access the scolari Website and the links given there. If, after reading this chapter, you want to know more how we use NVIVO, please feel free to contact us personally at our Website (http://members.aol.com/lbsilverst/fathers/index.html).

How to Do Bottom-Up Coding to Develop Theory

We will now examine how to use NVIVO to develop theory with bottom-up coding. Recall that you have no theoretical constructs when you begin bottom-up coding, and so must develop them while doing the data analysis. This is the method by which we analyzed the Haitian father data, and was discussed in chapters 5, 6, and 7.

The procedures of chapter 5, 6, and 7 are readily carried out with NVIVO. The method makes use of two types of NVIVO nodes: free nodes and tree nodes. Relevant text is first coded at a free node. Then a three-level coding tree is built. In the tree, level 1, the lowest level, codes repeating ideas, and levels 2 and 3 code themes and theoretical constructs. Thus, using the NVIVO terminology, repeating idea nodes are children of theme nodes, which in turn are children of theoretical construct nodes. This method is, of course, only one of many possible ways to code using NVIVO. You may develop your own methods, which you should feel free to use (and tell us about).

Begin your data analysis by opening an NVIVO project for the data that you want to analyze. Then import your interviews into the NVIVO project as rich text documents, making one document for each research group. For purposes of data analysis, we recommend that you make a new paragraph each time a new person speaks. Finally, create a research journal as an internal document. You will use your journal to record your thoughts about the data analysis.

Having done this, you are ready to begin analyzing the data.

Making the Text Manageable

Step 1: Explicitly state your research concerns and conceptual framework

This step requires no explanation: You carry it out the same way as when you analyzed the data by hand. We recommend that you enter your thoughts in your research journal.

Step 2: Select the relevant text for further analysis

The basic idea here is to code your relevant text in a free node. Do this using invivo coding, that is, coding directly from the text in the document browser.

1. Begin with group 1 and read through the text paragraph by paragraph. As you do so, you will be struck by words or phrase that signal relevant text. Highlight these words and then underline them by creating a databite, which you may annotate with the reason you found them relevant.
2. Highlight the words of the databite again and code them with invivo coding. You now have a free node with the words of the databite as a title.
3. Highlight the entire passage that contains text relevant to the databite and code it at the node you have just created. Use the speed coder for this. You now have the relevant text coded at the node.
4. Using the properties dialogue box, describe what the relevant text is about. This is particularly important, because you will later want to reference the description.
5. Continue this process with all of the text in all of the groups. When you are done, you will have relevant text coded at free nodes.

Note that as you are doing this you may find yourself using the same free node to code several different passages of text. This is fine, and, in fact, you are anticipating the next step, creating repeating ideas. As you code, you will probably have thoughts about where your data are going. Record them in your project journal.

Hearing What Was Said

Step 3: Record repeating ideas by grouping together related passages of relevant text

The basic idea here is to combine related passages of relevant text located at different free nodes into a single tree node that codes the idea they have in common, the repeating idea. When you did this by hand, you began with a list of all relevant text and then reduced the list by extracting relevant text. The same procedure can be carried out with NVIVO.

1. Using the tools menu, create a node set consisting of all your free nodes and title it "relevant text."
2. Using the tools menu again, print out all the relevant text nodes

and their description, using the "lists the nodes" option for the set. Save the report for future reference.

3. Read through this set of free nodes, using the starter text idea if necessary. When you find free nodes that go together, move them into a new set, and give this set a name that corresponds to the idea you think they express. You may need to browse the nodes to do this, or you may be able to do it from the descriptions. Once you have moved the free nodes to the new set, remove them from the list of relevant text. This will create a reduced list. The group of nodes transferred into your new set contains nodes that will become your first repeating idea. Keep track of what you are doing in your research journal, so you have a record of the idea.
4. Continue this process until the relevant text set is empty, making any necessary adjustments. You are now ready to start creating repeating ideas.
5. Take the first set and browse through the text that is associated with it. Name the text as in chapter 6, using a name that fits all the text. Record your thoughts in your project journal. You may want to create a memo for the process, which you will later link to the node.
6. When you have decided on a name, create a tree node with that name, and then merge the free nodes with that tree node. Use the copy operation, not the cut operation, so that you have a continued record of your relevant text for later inspection. Make sure that you have at least two different speakers for each repeating idea. If you don't, you can now go back to your original documents and find them, doing new coding as necessary. Make sure the idea is well described so that you can remember what you were thinking. You can also put longer thoughts in a memo.
7. Continue this process until you have used up all your free nodes, and therefore all your relevant text.
8. When you are finished, delete the sets. You will need the space.

Step 4. Organize themes by grouping repeating ideas into coherent categories

In this step you are going to create tree nodes for each theme. These free nodes will be parent nodes to the repeating ideas that define the theme.

The process is the same as with Step 3, that is, grouping the repeating ideas into themes by a process of selection. Consequently, our description will be somewhat abbreviated.

1. Print out a list of all your tree nodes so that you can inspect them. Also use the sets editor to create a set called "repeating ideas."
2. Go through the same operations as before, in which you inspect your set of repeating ideas, and group them into sets of nodes that cluster into a coherent category.
3. Each of these sets defines a theme. Inspect the free nodes, the repeating idea nodes, descriptions, and text, until you find a name for the theme.
4. Then create another free node with that name, and move the repeating ideas to be "children" of that node. Make sure you describe the theme node. You will probably want to record your thoughts in your research journal.
5. Continue this process, making adjustments as appropriate, until you have used all the repeating ideas.

Developing Theory

Step 5. Develop theoretical constructs by grouping themes into units consistent with your theoretical framework

The basic idea here is to tree nodes that correspond to theoretical constructs and therefore have the theme nodes as children. The mechanics of doing so are the same as in the previous step and need not be repeated here.

Having completed this step, you have created a coding tree that corresponds to our levels of data analysis. The highest level nodes code theoretical constructs; the middle level nodes code themes; and the lowest level nodes code repeating ideas. You can print the entire tree using the tools menu with the instruction "list all tree nodes."

Step 6. Create a theoretical construct by retelling the participant's story in terms of the theoretical constructs

The procedure for carrying out this step is, of course, the one described in chapter 6. It requires thought, rather than coding, and NVIVO cannot directly assist you with it. However, you might find it useful to use NVIVO to browse through your research journal, and collect your thoughts on the emerging story.

How to Do Top-Down Coding to Develop Theory

We will now examine how to use NVIVO to develop theory with top-down coding. Recall that top-down coding, or elaborative coding, begins with theoretical constructs and then develops themes and repeating ideas that flesh out the constructs. This is the method by which we analyzed the Promise Keepers data, and was discussed in chapter 10.

These procedures, too, are readily carried out with NVIVO. As was done with bottom-up coding, you create a three-level coding tree of theoretical constructs, themes, and repeating ideas. The procedures for creating the tree top-down are only slightly different from those for creating the tree bottom-up. Consequently, our description of the procedure will be brief, focusing only on the differences.

Making the Text Manageable

Step 1. Explicitly state your new research concerns, your theoretical constructs, and what you want to develop further

This step is done the same way as Step 1 for bottom-up coding.

Step 2. Select the relevant text for further analysis

This step is done the same way as for bottom-up coding, that is, browsing the text and creating free nodes for the relevant text. The only difference is that when you describe the free nodes, you should record the theoretical construct to which the node corresponds.

Hearing What Was Said

Step 3. Record repeating ideas by grouping together related passages of relevant text

This step is done the same way as for bottom-up coding, that is, creating a tree node for each repeating idea and then merging the free nodes of relevant text with the tree node. The only difference is that you know in advance that these repeating ideas will support a given theoretical construct, so you work only with the free nodes already grouped under that theoretical construct.

In addition, you may find that the relevant text suggests themes, so you can first group the relevant text nodes into themes and then construct repeating ideas that support the themes.

Step 4. Organize themes by grouping repeating ideas into coherent categories

This step is done the same way as for bottom-up coding, that is, creating a tree node corresponding to the theme, and making the repeating idea nodes children of that parent node. If you have constructed some tentative themes in Step 3, you can make use of them here.

Developing Theory

Step 5. Elaborate old theoretical constructs by grouping themes into units consistent with them

This step is done the same way as for bottom-up coding, that is, creating a tree node corresponding to the theoretical construct, and making the theme nodes children of the theoretical construct parent node.

Step 6. Create a theoretical narrative by retelling the participants' story in terms of the theoretical constructs

This step is done the same way as for bottom-up coding.

Appendix B

The Haitian American Fathers Study

Since the 1960s, mainstream discourse in both the social sciences and the popular press has characterized fatherhood among black men in U.S. culture primarily from a negative perspective (Biller, 1968; Moynihan, 1965). The "crisis of black men" has been linked to high rates of early childbearing, and marital separation and divorce. Hunter and Davis (1994) have pointed out that studies of black women have highlighted how adversity has generated creativity and resilience, whereas research on black men has emphasized emasculation and pathology. Similarly, mainstream research paradigms have minimized the diversity among black fathers, underlining role failure, rather than adaptation and strength. With some important exceptions (e.g., Hossain & Roopnarine, 1993; McAdoo, 1988, 1993) research on black fathers has focused primarily on the stresses of teen fatherhood (Kiselica, 1995, Robinson, 1988) and on father absence (e.g., McClanahan, 1986; Mott, 1994).

The current study presents an alternative to the negative stereotype of black men as uninvolved and/or irresponsible fathers. It describes a group of married, Haitian American fathers from diverse economic levels who are actively involved with their children. This study is part of a larger qualitative research project that documents the diversity of fatherhood identities within U.S. society. The goal of our fathering research is twofold: to provide a detailed description of the fathering practices of men from a variety of subcultures to maintain a high level of paternal involvement; and to develop middle level theories of father involvement. Middle level theories are based on a detailed analysis of a particular subculture, as opposed to high level theories, which are intended to apply to larger populations of many subcultures. We expect that the data will reveal a variety of strategies that successful fathers use, and a number of different family contexts and societal structures that support those strategies. We plan to elaborate this material into theoretical models for promoting involvement among men who have not yet found a way to become active, responsible fathers.

Our work originates from a model of feminist research which is consciously reflexive. Reflexivity is defined as a critical examination of the research process. Thus, we acknowledge that our interest in fathering emerges from a particular political perspective (Silverstein, 1996) in the intense social controversy surrounding responsible fatherhood. Many conservative social theorists have linked responsible fatherhood to marriage and the traditional nuclear family. They advocate reinstating a hierarchical family structure in which the father is the "leader" or "head" of the family, and the mother a valuable subordinate. Less conservative theorists have conceptualized the fathering role as independent of any particular family structure, and therefore assume that positive father involvement can exist within many different family forms.

Our theoretical model seeks to encourage father involvement with subordinating mothers or minimizing their importance. We define responsible fathering as behavior that is based on an emotional attachment to a child which is independent of the father's relationship to a child which is independent of the father's relation to the child's mother. Thus dissolution of that bond should not preclude continuing emotional attachment and active involvement between father and child. In addition, we believe that nurturing and caretaking are activities that are as integral to responsible fatherhood as to motherhood. Thus our broader agenda is to place attachment and nurturing at the center of the cultural definition of fathering, and, ultimately of masculine gender-role socialization.

We acknowledge that our subjectivity influences the way in which we conduct research. The two senior authors are both middle-aged, middle-class, white psychologists, trained in the positivist tradition. The third author is a young, middle-class Haitian American psychologist. We all have intense histories with our own fathers (and mothers) which undoubtedly have influenced our decision to study fatherhood. We are all parents, two of us have biological children, the other is a step-parent. We share this information because, in contrast to the positivist tradition, we know that the personal characteristics of the researchers are relevant to research process and findings (Allen & Walker, 1992).

This article presents a detailed description of the subjective experiences of a group of Haitian American fathers, using their own words and concepts. We discuss our findings in relation to a metatheory about the transformation of fathering which is occurring within U.S. culture. This theory proposes four components which are necessary for role change: a sense of personal dissatisfaction with current role norms; a new set of behaviors which provide a sense of personal gratification; a facilitating ideology which prescribes the new behaviors and proscribes the old ones; and a supportive community which provides a system of social supports to help manage the anxiety that is an inevitable consequence of change. We believe that the data support our first two theoretical constructs, indicating that these Haitian Christian fathers have constructed a new definition of fatherhood which is more socially progressive and more personally satisfying than the traditional Haitian fathering role. We will speculate about the constructs of ideology and community which we believe have contributed to this transformation of fatherhood, but which are not clearly reflected in the data. We conclude with a suggestion about the importance of integrating both qualitative and quantitative designs into social science research.

Methodology

The Qualitative Research Paradigm

Hunter and Davis (1994) have pointed out that, because black men have been defined exclusively in relation to white male privilege, relatively little is known about how black men define themselves. The qualitative paradigm is particularly well suited to investigate voices and perspectives from nondominant cultures about which very little is known. Qualitative researchers explicitly acknowledge that their status as researcher puts them in the privileged position of member of the dominant culture and its definition of reality. This is especially true when the researchers are ethnically part of the dominant group, as are the senior authors. Therefore, qualitative researchers try to structure data collection collaboratively. Rather than imposing the researcher's assumptions, participants are encouraged to use their own voices and to articulate their own experiences. Because qualitative research is neither as widely understood, nor as generally accepted, as a quantitative approach, we begin with a brief description of the general assumptions underlying a qualitative model, and then describe the particular variant that we used.

The goal of qualitative research is to generate *thick description* (Geertz, 1973, 1983), that is, the explication and detailed description of the world of the people who live out the phenomenon one is investigating. The descriptive material can then be analyzed to yield *sensitizing concepts* which articulate categories by which people understand their own world. Qualitative research develops grounded theory, that is, theoretical constructs, derived from and grounded in, the participant's own understanding (Strauss & Corbin, 1990) The grounded theory can then be used to generate specific hypotheses which can be examined quantitatively.

Although there are differences in particular methods used by qualitative researchers, most share the same general procedure (Dey, 1993; Miles & Huberman, 1994). Qualitative research begins with a set of texts produced by members of a culture as they talk about, and reflect on, a social phenomenon. The participant's own subjectivity and definition of the situation are reflected in these texts, which constitute the data of the qualitative analysis. The goal of qualitative research is to use the researcher's own subjectivity in a disciplined way, in order to enter into and interpret the cultural world of the text. In older, ethnographic, traditions this understanding was then expressed in the form of an interpretive narrative. More recently, however, researchers aim at expressing their understanding by developing a structured system of categories that are coordinated with the text, and with each other (Richards & Richards, 1994).

Although there is not a mechanical recipe from extracting a category system from text, analysis generally includes three levels of categories; text-driven categories, coherence-driven categories, and theory-driven constructs (Miles & Huberman, 1994; Richards & Richards, 1994). Text-driven categories become visible because research participants often use relatively equivalent words and phrases. As the text-based category system develops, the researcher becomes aware that these lower level categories stand in logical or conceptual relation to each other, and therefore can be organized into coherence-based categories. The researcher then uses theoretical concepts from the research literature or from their own hypotheses to organize the coherence-based categories into theory-driven constructs.

Research Participants

The research participants were 20 Haitian American men recruited from a single Haitian Baptist church in Brooklyn, New York. Many of the men knew each other and the moderator, who was also a member of this church. All the participants had been born in Haiti, and had immigrated to the United States sometime during their teenage or early adult years. They all spoke English, French, and Creole. The men had been raised in a variety of family structures. The majority had been raised in a family with two parents, although some had been raised primarily by their mothers. Three of the men has seen their fathers leave their mothers for other women, or have children with other women while remaining married. Two of the men stated that they had never known their father.

Demographic information is summarized in Table B.1. The ages of the men ranged from 29 to 60, with a mean age of 40. They had been married from 2 to 34 years, and had from 1 to 5 children. Most of the men had graduated from high school. All of the men were employed, except for one who was a full-time student. Their income ranged from $0 to $70,000. With a mean income of $38,800. The frequency distribution of income and education shown in Table B.1 indicate that the sample is very diverse.

Focus Group Procedure

The guided conversation which constituted the research interview was conducted in a focus group format. Focus groups were used because they sample the experiences of a wide variety of subjects in a relatively easy fashion. Focus groups provide an opportunity for participants to report their individual experiences, and also respond to the experiences of other group members. Consequently, new information can emerge that is not available from researcher-designed survey instruments, individual interviews, or participant observation (Morgan, 1988).

Table B.1
A Frequency Distribution of the Participants by Age, Education, and Income

Category	*N*	%
Age		
20–29	1	(5)
30–39	12	(60)
40–49	3	(15)
50–59	3	(15)
60–69	1	(5)
Total	20	(100)
Income (in $1,000)		
0–15	4	(20)
16–30	9	(45)
31–50	4	(20)
51–70	3	(15)
Total	20	(100)
Education		
Less than High School	4	(20)
12	3	(15)
13–15	7	(35)
16+	6	(30)
Total	20	(100)

The third author was the moderator of all of the focus groups. He asked the men six questions which took them through a narrative account of their fathering experiences; (1) When was the first time you thought about being a father, and what did you think it would be like? (2) What is your relationship with your father, and how has it affected your fathering? (3) How did you and your wife go through the process of deciding to have a child? (4) What is being a father like? How did it change your sense of who you are, and what your life is about? What are you most proud of, and what do you most regret? (6) How has being a father affected your relationship with your parents and siblings? Following this, the men were invited to share any thoughts they had not as yet voiced.

Five focus groups were conducted. Each group lasted approximately 1 1/2–2 hours. The groups ranged in size from three to six participants. The group discussion was videotaped and transcribed. The transcribed interviews formed the text for data analysis. Some of the questions yielded responses more relevant to the concerns of this article than others, and consequently are over represented in our data analysis.

Data Analysis

We have used three levels of data analysis, (1) low level, text-based categories; (2) middle level sensitizing concepts, and (3) high level theoretical constructs. The procedure does not develop linearly from low to high level because the categories are continually revised to reflect the researcher's evolving interpretation of the text. However, for purposes of exposition, we shall present our process of data analysis as if it were more or less sequential.

After all the focus groups had been conducted, and the texts of each group transcribed, the texts were read over by four members of our research group—the third author, another graduate student, and the senior authors. Working independently, each researcher selected segments of text which were seen as relevant to the basic concerns of the study. This selection process consisted of recording key words, phrases, and passages, which the participants themselves had repeated or otherwise indicated as important ideas. Each researcher then developed a set of Level One text-based categories which paraphrased or generalized the text itself. For example, many of the participants said that their fathering experiences had changed them in terms of becoming more responsible and mature. We used on of their quotes, *It has changed you: it has reconstructed you,* to represent this text-based category.

The list of sensitizing concepts was developed in a similar manner. Again, working independently, each researcher organized the text-based categories into clusters of Level Two sensitizing concepts (see Table B.2). These reflected tacit or explicit themes that were closed enough to the text that they should be recognizable to the research participants. For example, the Level One category cited above, *It has changed you; it has reconstructed you,* was grouped along with another similar idea under the more general sensitizing concept of *An enhanced sense of self.*

Because the subjective experiences of men from nondominant subcultures are relatively unknown to mainstream psychology, two outside researchers are always included in our data analysis of each fathering

Table B.2

Theoretical Constructs, Sensitizing Concepts, and Text-Based Categories

I. Bicultural gender role strain	
A. Praising aspects of the traditional Haitian father	50%
1. My dream was to look like my father.	
2. There is no inch of laziness in my father.	
3. I love the way my father treated my mother.	
B. Dissatisfactions with aspects of traditional Haitian fatherhood	60%
4. My father never said I love you.	
5. Adults do not play.	
6. When they say your father is coming you run inside.	
7. My father took care of other children and didn't care much for me.	
II. Constructing a more gratifying definition of fatherhood	
A. Definition of a "good" father.	100%
8. My job is to look over the family.	
9. You're not a boss for the children, you're more like a friend.	
10. You have to be there whenever the child needs you.	
11. You call your kid and say I love you.	
12. Jesus was my role model.	
B. An enhanced sense of self.	75%
13. It has changed you, it has reconstructed you.	
14. You've looking at the children growing it is beautiful	
III. A facilitating ideology	
A. God makes all things possible.	75%
15. We are co-workers in the field of God.	
16. It won't be your doing, it will be God's doing.	

Note: N=20. The percentages refer to the percentage of fathers in the sample who used the sensitizing concept.

subculture. In the case of Haitian fathers, another male Haitian graduate student and a male African American psychologist each coded one transcript into text-based categories and a list of sensitizing concepts. The data analyses of the outside raters were then added to the category list of the research group.

The research group then met together to compare and contrast each researcher's organization of the data. The lists of key words, phrases, and passages were uniform across researchers. The Level One, text-based categories were likewise very similar. The most diversity existed among the lists of sensitizing concepts, but even here, there was overlap among researchers. The outside raters added new perspectives to the data analysis, which led to the further revision of the category system. For example, the Haitian graduate student deepened our understanding of the respect the men had for their own fathers. He also called our attention to the generational, as well as cultural, changes in the fathering role. After extensive discussion a single, comprehensive list of text-based categories and sensitizing concepts was established by group consensus. In the original analysis if the data, the third author organized a subset of sensitizing concepts into a set of theoretical constructs that derive from our metatheory of social change.

Although the number of categories is in principle arbitrary, we find that we can capture the essence of a text in from 25 to 40 Level One categories. Similarly, it is our experience that 10–15 sensitizing concepts (about one-third of the previous level) adequately reflect the sense of the data. Because of space considerations, we have not presented the full array of categories. However, the complete data set is available from the authors.

Reliability and Validity

Qualitative research addresses the issues of reliability and validity in a way that contrasts with a quantitative approach. As suggested by Rubin & Rubin (1995), we have established a procedure which is *transparent* (another investigator can know and check what we have done; *communicable* (the categories made sense to both the participants themselves, and to other investigators who want to use them); and *coherent* (the categories were simultaneously internally consistent, as well as reflective of both individual differences and genuine inconsistencies in the culture).

We have tried to achieve these goals by incorporating multiple raters at each stage of the research process. As an additional check on our interpretation of the text, we went to the church where the original focus groups had been held, and met with 10 of the 20 men who had participated in the study. This meeting occurred about six months after data collection. We presented the text-based categories and sensitizing concepts. In the ensuing discussion, the men confirmed the accuracy of our sensitizing concepts. Many of them commented, "I could have said that." Others stated, "That is exactly how I feel." They also sharpened our understanding of two of our theoretical constructs; their complex feelings about their own fathers and the traditional Haitian fathering role, and the role of religion and the church in their definition of fatherhood. We believe that presenting the researcher's understanding of the data to the participants is essential in assuring the validity of the findings, especially when members of the research team are not members of the culture being studied.

Results

In this section, we present our text-driven categories and sensitizing concepts. Table B.2 illustrates the way in which the text-drive categories logically cluster into sensitizing concepts. The sensitizing concepts are presented here as subsection headings, and the text-driven categories as paragraph headings. Table B.2 also indicates our organization of the sensitizing concepts into higher order theoretical constructs, which will be presented below in the discussion section.

Praising Aspects of the Traditional Haitian Father

My Dream Was to Look like My Father

As Table B.2 indicates, 50% of the fathers explicitly praised aspects of traditional Haitian fatherhood. These men admired their fathers' strength and sense of responsibility. They report that their fathers were positive role models for them.

> *C:* . . . When I think of the days of my youth I can see my father and his dedication. The love that he has shown, and his hard working style, and his honesty. All that, they left a serious imprint on me. My dream was to look like my father. (Zizi, 1996, p. 221)
>
> *L:* My father was a very good father. He is a guy who has justice. You cannot make him tremble in situations. . . . (Zizi, 1996, p. 170)

I Love the Way My Father Treated My Mother

> *F:* I love the way my father used to treat my mother. . . . When we were going through some difficult times, he was kind of an emotional leader to keep us together by bringing something that would make us happy. (Zizi, 1996, p. 171)

There Is No Inch of Laziness in My Father

> *T:* My father is extremely responsible. He will take time for his family. It does not matter what he has to do. There is no inch of laziness in my father. (Zizi, 1996, p. 177)

Dissatisfactions with Aspects of Traditional Haitian Father

In addition to the aspects of their fathers that the men admired, 60% of the men also expressed a variety of dissatisfactions about the way their fathers had behaved. The first two categories reflect their unhappiness with their fathers' emotional distance

My Father Never Said I Love You

This subgroup reported that their fathers were not emotionally demonstrative, neither giving nor allowing expressions of love. The men recognized that this was culturally determined, and felt that the love was there, even though their fathers could not express it directly. All of the men in the current study reported that this was something they wanted to change. They wanted to express their love to their children directly and often.

> *AG:* Sometimes we cannot go to our father and say to our father, you know something, I love you.
>
> *F:* Yeah, it is part of our culture. For me especially, even though I never heard such a word from my father's mouth such as I love you, the way they act to us and the way they deal with us makes me feel like definitely this guy loves me.
>
> *L:* I tell you my father also never uttered the word I love you. . . . But you knew he did. I make corrections in my family. I must repeat to my children, I love them, I do not know, every several hours. Maybe every one hour. (Zizi, 1996, p. 179)

Adults Do Not Play

These men also reported that neither their fathers nor their mothers recognized play as a part of Haitian parenting. Several said that they felt unhappy about the absence of informality and playfulness in their relationship with their fathers, and wanted to create a different emotional tone with their own children.

> *F:* There is one bad thing that I did not like about my father. I have to bring it up. I do not know how to play any sports. I will never learn how to play since my father never played with me. So I think I am trying my best to learn as much as I can, because I play with my kids. I take them out whenever I have the time.
>
> *ET:* I think we could say that for most of us, the Haitian father figure is supposed to be strict, stern, strong figure, not to show any signs of weakness. No play, as they say, "Gran moun pa jouwe" [Adults do not play]. (Zizi, 1996, p. 180)

Sometimes the sternness in their father's attitude was associated with authoritarianism and physical force. Many of the men found their fathers to be excessively strict. However, they also believed that strictness was a necessary component of good fathering. F and L below discuss the complexity of their attitudes toward discipline and corporal punishment.

When They Say Your Father Is Coming, You Run Inside

> *F:* My father would beat the hell out of me if I did something wrong.
>
> *L:* There was no such thing as playing around. So I always had someone watching to see when my father appeared at the end of the block. All they had to say is, "your father is coming," and I would run inside. Every once in a while he would catch me playing and I would be in trouble. (Laughs).

Another group member asks whether F will spank has daughter.

> *F:* Definitely I will. I think that spanking can help later in life. I'm not saying that. I will beat the hell out of my kid, but I will talk to my kid first. I realize that before you spank the kid, you must let her know why she is getting spanked. This is one of the things my father did not do. (Zizi, 1996, p. 176)

My Father Took Care of Other Children and Didn't Care Much for Me

One of the cultural aspects of Haitian fatherhood that all the men rejected was the tradition of having children in the context of relationships with several women. A small percentage of the men had experienced this with their own fathers.

> *A:* My father had only me with my mother, then he got married and took care of other children and didn't care much for me, which is why I never had any relationship with him. (Zizi, 1996, p. 139)

One of the older men (aged 60) had fathered a child without being married. This had occurred in Haiti, before he had become a Christian. He describes his experience.

> *R:* Naturally, it wasn't God's will. We did contrary to the will of God, which is why I have a child with her prior to marriage. That is a biblical violation. (Zizi, 1996, p. 134)

Defining a "Good" Father

All (100%) of the men were concerned with becoming a "good" father. Three major ideas characterized the men's fathering ideal: being a responsible provider and protector; being less authoritarian than their own fathers had been; and being physically present and affectionate with their children.

My Job Is to Look Over the Family, Being a Provider, a Protector

All of the men agreed on this traditional aspect of fathering. Being a good father was a heavy responsibility, involving the traditional roles of provider and protector. The following quote gives the flavor of their experience.

> *DE:* Being a father to me is a full time job, and beyond that. I find myself thinking about my family constantly, even at work. I'm thinking about the next thing to do for them, how could I provide best for them. I'm worried

> about their safety, calling constantly, worried about their whereabouts. . . . My job is to look over the family, being a provider, provider, a protector. It is like being a guard. (Zizi, 1996, p. 233)

You're Not a Boss for the Children, You're More like a Friend

Although all of the men, as we have seen, took on the traditional patriarchal role, most of them liberalized and qualified it, becoming a father who did not tyrannize his children. The following quote illustrates this change. The first speaker noted that this less authoritarian stance is a cultural change, which he attributed to being in the United States rather than in Haiti.

> *M:* . . . As a father in the new generation and as a Christian and someone who has had the opportunity to go to school and receive an education, I believe that I made a great effort to accept and understand the importance of recreation with my children. . . . You are not a boss for children telling them to do this or that, you're more like a friend who takes them to the park, plays with them. It (the old form of fatherhood) results from being raised in a Third World country. In those countries these things are priorities, but here in the U.S., play is extremely important for the child's development. (Zizi, 1996, p. 249)

You Call Your Kid and Say I Love You

> *AG:* As a Haitian father, I would like kind of to enhance . . . that you make sure that when you have your kind, you call your kid and say "I love you," even if the kid is 20 or 22 (Zizi, 1996, p. 179)

> *L:* There is not a day that passes that I do not kiss Morahia. You probably see me kissing her in church. . . . (Zizi, 1996, p. 179)

You Have to Be There Whenever the Child Needs You

> *A:* When you have a child, there are certain times that you have to invest, spending time with the child. You have to be there for the child whenever the child needs you. (Zizi, 1996, p. 207)

H: I am always there for my kids. Like all of last week, I change the shift on my job so I can be there for the kids. (Zizi, 1996, p. 159)

Jesus Was My Role Model

We have seen references to God threaded through the men's descriptions of their ideas about fathering. Many of the men stated that they explicitly tried to model their behavior on Jesus.

A: I saw the bad experience that my father had. He couldn't support his Children. As a result, the children did whatever they wanted to do. They came in whenever they wanted, living a terrible life in the home. . . . I knew I would be married, I would have children and I had to take care of my kids.

Moderator: Who was your model?

A: Well, I can say in my life, I didn't have a model. Jesus was my model. (Zizi, 1996, p. 138)

An Enhanced Sense of Self

All of the men expressed great personal satisfaction in their own fathering. They reported that fathering has transformed their lives in the direction of greater maturity.

It Has Changed You: It Has Reconstructed You

G: It has changed your life completely, you have a sense of responsibility. You do not think the same way, you cannot act the same way. You are everything for the child, not only are you the child's friend, but you have to know when you have to be strict. At one point you have to be strict and soft. . . . It is a big responsibility, it has changed you, it has reconstructed you. (Zizi, 1996, p. 263)

P: When I was a younger person, I was kind of care free. You know, one who likes to go out, like the stuff that teenagers do without thinking. But being a father, you know that you have a family to take care of, to provide for. It makes you think twice before you do anything, so my lifestyle has changed. (Zizi, 1996, p. 197)

P: Being a father is a great privilege. Before I was married. I used to feel worthless—that I would rather die than live. . . . (Zizi, 1996, pp. 259–260)

FR: What brings me joy is that God gave me the courage, the strength and opportunity to assume my responsibility as a father. . . . My way of carrying myself changed. I've become a leader because the children that are growing up have to follow me. . . . (Zizi, 1996, p. 164)

You're Looking at the Children Growing. It Is Beautiful

The men also express great pride and satisfaction in the whole experience of having children, as the following dialogue between the moderator and a father illustrates.

Moderator: What are you most proud of?

G: So! Me, I'm proud to see the children playing and you see it is you, It is yours, you made them. You're looking at the children growing. It is beautiful.

Moderator: What do you most regret?

G: There are no regrets. I'm glad about the whole experience, my children, that's beautiful. (Zizi, 1996, p. 264)

God Makes All Things Possible

For these men, much of their life is centered in religion. All of these men identified themselves as Christians. All of the men experienced God as an active force in their lives, taking care of them and governing the basic aspects of their life. The following quotes illustrate this conception of God, and the close relation between their religious beliefs and their family life.

We Are Co-Workers in the Field of God

C: After I got married, our relationship with God as children of God, and ourselves having children, I learned that God has a plan, and He wants us to be a co-worker in the field. (Zizi, 1996, p. 228)

C: Being a man is like being small god. You have a chance to form someone . . . to bring up a young mind. (Zizi, 1996, p. 229)

It Won't Be Your Doing, It Will Be God's Doing

AF: On the . . . point of economics, God never puts you in a situation where He would not provide. He always takes care of his children, my self being one. It changes me in a way, it gives more understanding. (Zizi, 1996, p. 229)

R: . . . each child she carries, the doctor always told her she would not survive. I told her, "as long as you are pregnant, God will always spare your life." When she became pregnant with Rudy, she had decided to abort. Her blood count was so low, she became very pale. I said, "honey, leave the baby right where it is at. . . . God will make the birth occur. It won't be your doing, it will be God's doing." (Zizi, 1996, pp. 134–135)

Discussion

The final stage in the development of grounded theory requires that we organized our sensitizing concepts into theoretical constructs that illuminate the transformation of fatherhood. In our view, this is both a "top down" and a "bottom up" process. It is top down because we use a metatheory to guide the organization of the sensitizing concepts. It is bottom up because the theory must be supported by the sensitizing concepts.

Our metatheory addresses the issues of cultural role change. The structure of fatherhood is evolving in U.S. culture. Some groups are departing from the traditional definition altogether. Other men are maintaining or updating many aspects of the traditional role. Some changes are in the direction of power-sharing and role flexibility; while other modifications serve to maintain patriarchy and a more traditional sexual division of labor. Our metatheory focuses on the change process. It contains four constructs which we believe are necessary for change to occur: an internal sense of dissatisfaction with the old role norms; a new way of behaving that is experienced as personally satisfying, an ideology that prescribes new behaviors and proscribes old ones; and a system of social supports for managing the anxiety that inevitably accompanies change. Although it may seem as if these four constructs reflect changes that occur sequentially, or are in linear relation to each other, actually, these ideas represent phenomena that are interrelated, overlapping, and circular.

In this study, we found data to support the first two constructs, but not latter two. The sense of dissatisfaction with the old social organization we have called *bicultural gender role strain*. The new definition of fatherhood which is a more satisfying way of behaving we have called *constructing a more gratifying fatherhood*. Table B.2 shows these constructs, and the sensitizing concepts that they subsume. Table B.2 also presents one sensitizing concept that relates to the third construct, a facilitating ideology. Data relating to the other aspect of ideology, economic necessity, and to the fourth theoretical construct, a supportive community, did not emerge in the current study. We present these latter ideas as hypotheses to be tested in future research.

Theory Driven Constructs

Bicultural Gender Role Strain

Pleck (1981, 1995) has argued that gender roles always contain Prescriptions for behaviors that are mutually contradictory and internally inconsistent. Thus, attempting to conform to gender role expectations inevitably generates internal conflict and gender role strain. Gender role strain for these Haitian American fathers emerges from two primary sources; ideological and personal. For all of the men in the current study, Haitian culture was their original frame of reference. Thus, they were very much affected by Haitian fatherhood ideology. However, all of the men have lived in the United States for an extended period of time, that is, from 10 to 20 years. Most of them married and became fathers in the United States. Thus, they have also been acculturated to U.S. fatherhood ideology. This bicultural experience has created a particular version of gender role strain.

The majority of the men expressed disappointment in the emotional distance characteristic of their relationship with their own fathers. They wanted to be very different from their own fathers in terms of their emotional attachment to their children. Yet, most of the men loved and respected their fathers and used them as role models. These conflicting feelings about their own fathers caused a more personal version of gender role strain. We will present the contrasting ideologies of the traditional Haitian father and the more nurturant U.S. father, and discuss the men's personal experience of role conflict and strain.

The traditional Haitian fathering role defined the father as the authoritarian head of the family, with control over mother and children (Bastien, 1951; Durand, 1980; Lasry & Frédérik, 1986). Gender roles were constructed by a rigid division of labor. The father was either the sole or primary provider. Household management and child care was left almost exclusively to mothers and other women (maids, aunts, grandmothers). Bastien (1951) gives an example of the rigidity of the sexual division of labor by describing the practice of wives hiring other women to help out in the home when they were ill, because husbands were unwilling to mind children or do simple chores. Even in matters of discipline, fathers were consulted only in the context of extreme transgressions.

Despite his lack of involvement in child care and household management, the father was considered the head of the family. Corporal punishment was used liberally by both mothers and fathers, because a child was considered "un petit animal" [a little animal] who must be tamed, and taught how to behave in society (Durand, 1980, p. 48). Bastien (1951) concluded that Haitian families represented an extreme version of patriarchy. "Le pouvoir paternal etait indiscute" [The father's power was indisputable] (p. 23). A sexual double standard existed which considered extramarital relationships the norm among men, but provided legal punishment to women who committed adultery. Therefore, it was common for men to have children with several women. Children were not allowed to marry without their father's consent, and they often remained under his authority throughout their adulthood.

A less extreme version of the traditional, patriarchal fathering role also is present in U.S. culture. However, gender ideology in the United States has recently prescribed an alternative, nurturing version of fathering primarily in the context of a more role-sharing, egalitarian family structure. Although there is considerable debate about the extent to which this role definition is myth or reality (LaRossa, 1988, Silverstein, 1996), the idea of a caregiving father has become a cultural image. This popular ideal of the "nurturant" father defines the fathering role as more affectionate and more actively involved than the traditional Haitian father.

In the United States, the majority of mothers are engaged in paid employment. This requires that fathers be present and assume some of the responsibility for child care and household management. Thus fathers in the role-sharing model are involved in the care and activities of children in a way that is very different from the traditional Haitian father. In addition to being actively involved, nurturing fathers typically express affection, both physically and verbally. This affectionate stance defines a relationship of emotional closeness, rather than the emotional distance that was prevalent among the participants and their own fathers.

The sensitizing concept, ***dissatisfactions with the traditional Haitian fathering role,*** reflects the men's unhappiness with the authoritarian posture of their own fathers, and their determination to do things differently with their own children. The idea that ***adults don't play*** captured the formality of the traditional Haitian father and the emotional inaccessibility which the traditional Haitian father and the emotional inaccessibility which the men experienced with their fathers. These fathers made sure that they were physically present and involved with their children, and they expressed their affection physically and verbally. One of the fathers in the feedback session illustrated how dramatic this shift has been. He described his reaction as his children reached over and began eating from his breakfast plate.

> I was so happy—you can't get inside of me to understand how happy I was—because in my family, the food would be sitting on the table, but no one could eat until my father came home.

Another characteristic of traditional Haitian fathering which these men have given up is the practice of having children in multiple unions. Roopnarine and Benetti (1996) have indicated how widespread this behavior is in Caribbean culture. In a recent survey of all of the countries in the English-speaking Caribbean, these authors reported that 25% of the fathers were in "friending," or visiting relationships, and 20% were in common law marriages. Among men between the ages of 35 and 54, only 23% the fathers were married. The authors note that these patterns have been stable for over 150 years. The men in the current study, in contrast, have shifted away from these Caribbean role norms. All but one of the men have children in the context of only one marital union, and all of the men are resident with their children.

It is important to remember, however, that the men have not rejected, or even revised, every aspect of traditional Haitian fatherhood. The sensitizing concept, *praising aspects of the traditional Haitian father,* reflects the many ways in which these men admire their own fathers and want to be like them. The older generation of fathers communicated a sense of responsibility and a commitment to hard work which the younger men respect. In addition, the men continue to believe that some form of discipline is an important element of socialization for children, and thus an essential component to responsible fatherhood.

Thus, the current study indicates the complexity of integrating role norms from two cultural traditions. The men continually express ambivalence about whether they should define themselves as more similar to the traditional Haitian father or to the U.S. nurturing father. Their attitudes toward discipline reflect the strain that they are experiencing. Many of the men recalled their upset at being spanked by their fathers, and declared that they wanted to establish a less authoritarian stance with their own children. They wanted to assume the more democratic, U.S., ideal of being a friend, rather than a boss, to their children. Yet we also saw echoes of the more traditional idea that children must be "tamed," when the men talked about the importance of discipline in later life. The attempt to integrate these two contrasting cultural ideologies generated the somewhat incongruous idea that spanking is acceptable, as long as an explanation is given to the child.

This ambivalence about parenting ideology was accompanied by internal conflict about criticizing their fathers. On one hand, virtually all of the men spoke about the pain associated with the emotional distance they felt from their own fathers. On the other hand, many of them seemed uncomfortable rejecting their father's way of doing things. The depth of this ambivalence was expressed in the discussion that occurred in the feedback session. One father stated, "I can never remember sitting down and having a conversation with my father. I don't want my kids to say that." One of the fathers echoed this concern when he stated that his love for his father had always been tinged with dread. However, another man expressed the other side of the ambivalence by responding that dread was necessary in order to instill respect in children. One of the men defended the older generation, explaining that their values were appropriate for a Third World country. Still another argued that being strict must have been the best way because they (the men themselves) had turned out so well.

Thus, these fathers faced a number of interesting dilemmas. They believed that it was necessary for their children to respect and perhaps even dread them; yet they wanted to have a close, affectionate relationship with their kids. These fathers wanted their children to see them as emotionally accessible, yet they reserved the right to use physical punishment if the children were not obedient. Similarly, they wanted to do things differently than their fathers, yet they seemed to feel guilty criticizing them, and held on to the idea that their fathers' way was the "best way." Given the role strain that these conflicting feelings generated, it is not surprising that some of the men concluded, "I would go back to the old way," if it would work in U.S. society.

Constructing a More Gratifying Fatherhood

If we compare the men's definition of "a good father" with the traditional Haitian definition of the fathering role, we see that these fathers have maintained certain elements of the traditional role, and also made significant changes in the direction of the "nurturant" model. The traditional roles of provider and protector have been preserved in this new model of fatherhood. Supporting their children financially continued to provide a sense of self-esteem for these men. However, these fathers wanted to give up the authoritarian stance typical of their own fathers. For example, the men stated that they did not want to be a "boss" to their children, they wanted to establish the more democratic and emotionally connected relationship of a "friend." Although they were not completely consistent in choosing to give up this authoritarian style, as their discussion about spanking suggests, still the desire to be less hierarchical was a recurring theme.

The sensitizing concept, *enhanced sense of self,* summarizes the happiness and fulfillment the men experienced from having children. Throughout the groups, the men expressed a profound feeling of pride in their children, "You're looking at the children growing; it is beautiful." Although they spoke about having less time alone with their wives, overall, they reported feeling no regrets about becoming fathers.

They also stated that becoming a father had increased their sense of responsibility. Prior to becoming a father, some of the men reported living only for themselves—staying out late, not letting anyone know where they were or what they were doing. After their children arrived, they realized that they were also living for someone else. This realization led them to change their behavior in terms of staying home more, taking fewer risks, and monitoring their interactions with their wives, so that the children did not observe arguing and conflict. One of the men felt the change had been so profound that he described being "reconstructed."

The profound importance of the fathering experience for this group of men is illustrated in the declaration of one man, who stated that he felt worthless and unwilling to live until he became a father. A similar existential shift is reflected in the religious ideology of this group of Haitian Christian men. Children are seen as gifts from God, and through them God is experienced as actively involved in everyday life. As the men struggled to behave in a manner that was morally correct, they identified with Jesus which gave them strength and courage. Thus, their fatherhood experience provided them with a sense of higher purpose, that is, doing God's will.

From our theoretical perspective, we believe that the traditional male role, in both Haitian and U.S. culture, socializes men to be out of touch with their feelings and emotionally isolated from their families and from other men (Levant & Kopecky, 1995). Thus, we are predisposed to believe that active fathering provides a degree of emotional closeness to children which is in itself gratifying and reinforcing of behavioral change.

Implications for Further Research

We believe that the data support our first two theoretical constructs, indicating that these Haitian Christian fathers have constructed a new definition of fatherhood which is more socially progressive and more personally satisfying than the traditional Haitian fathering role. In this section, we will speculate about the constructs of ideology and community, which we believe have contributed to this transformation of fatherhood, but which are not clearly reflected in the data. We conclude with a suggestion about the importance of integrating both qualitative and quantitative designs into social science research.

A Facilitating Ideology

We were struck by the importance of the men's religious beliefs in defining their fathering behavior. The sensitizing concept, *God makes all things possible,* reflected the link between fatherhood and divinity. We speculate that their religious beliefs serve two functions. On one hand, using Jesus as a role model may provide a substitute ideology that allowed the men to give up some of the authoritarian aspects of the traditional patriarchal role. On the other had, their sense of connection to divine omnipotence may serve to manage anxiety about change, and also maintain some of the power associated with the more traditional patriarchal role.

Feminist theologians have pointed out that, in contrast to the "male warrior God" of the old testament (Plaskow, 1990, p. 131), Jesus preached a religion of love, compassion, and mercy (Fiorenza, 1979). The nurturing aspects of Jesus as an alternative vision of God is a strong tradition in the Christian church. For example, women who were leaders in defining medieval Christian spirituality referred to "Mother Jesus" (McLaughlin, 1979, p. 101). Thus, identifying with Jesus may have simultaneously allowed the fathers in our study to maintain their position as a powerful leader in the family while at the same time encouraging them to be less dominating.

As we have seen, the ideology of the "nurturant father" was not totally comfortable for these men. Although the concept of being emotionally close to their children was appealing, they were not yet ready to embrace a consistently democratic parenting style. For the men in the current study, their Christian theology seems to have presented them with moral code in the context of a definition of masculinity that was less focused on domination. Yet, it did not require them to relinquish male privilege entirely, because, as one man reminded us. "Being a man is like being a small god."

The current study did not examine directly the content of their religious ideology, and therefore our speculations about the ways in which it contributed to behavior change are not grounded in theory. We plan to include participant observation, such as spending time in church and in discussion groups, in our next study. In this way, we hope to test the accuracy of our hypotheses about the role of religion in supporting change.

A Community That Supports Active Fathering

Behavior change, even change that is desired and positive, always generates anxiety. Thus, in addition to a new ideology, people also need a system of social supports to bind the anxiety that is an inevitable consequence of change. We believe that the men's involvement in their church may have provided them with a socially supportive atmosphere which validated their new behaviors, and helped them manage their anxiety as they transformed their fathering role.

In the feedback session with 10 of the men, we asked them if belonging to the church provided them with a social community that was helpful to them on parenting issues. One of the men said that he and his wife met informally with other couples from the church to discuss marital and parenting issues. Overall, however, the men responded that they felt the church needed to do more. They wanted to begin parenting classes and discussion groups. They explained that being a good Christian was the first step in becoming a good parent, but was not sufficient. They expressed a strong desire to have the kind of support groups we had assumed the church community was already providing.

In the current study, we believe that the church community is already providing some support to the men in changing their fathering behaviors. Coming to church every Sunday may provide the men with the opportunity to observe and interact with other men who are committed to marriage and to active fathering. Although the men express the desire for even more support, we hypothesize that belonging to the church community validates their behavior and absorbs some degree of anxiety. The presence of informal groups further suggests that the church community provides peer relationships within which these fathers can confirm their commitment to a shared ideology. However the design of the current study did not address these hypotheses. Thus, the role of the church community in the transformation of fatherhood will be explored in the next study.

Limitations of the Research

There are several limitations inherent in the design of this study. First, the data were collected in group interviews, which allowed the expression of collective themes, but precluded more in-depth personal explorations of these themes. This was particularly true because the participants and the moderator were all members of the same church. Thus the participants were known to each other and to the moderator. This lack of anonymity may have motivated some of the participants to withhold important information, or to express more agreement with group norms than they actually felt. Despite the fact that the focus groups were not tightly structured, and spontaneous interaction between participants in the groups was encouraged, data collection was structured by researcher-designed questions. Because the results are similarly structured by those questions, important aspects of the men's fathering experiences may not be included in the findings.

The study is also limited by the fact that the data are self-report data. The men describe their cultural attitudes and behaviors, as elicited by our particular focus group interview. There may be many missing links between attitudes and behavior. To enumerate the most obvious; reported attitudes may differ from actual attitudes, reported behaviors may not correspond. Clearly, reports about behavior are not equivalent to direct observations.

In addition, these results cannot be generalized to all Haitian American fathers, or to all Haitian Christian fathers. All of the research participants were volunteers. Thus, they represent a self-selected sample of men who were willing to talk about their fathering experiences. They may differ in important ways from other Haitian American men, or even from other men in the same church who were not as interested in fathering, or who were not comfortable sharing personal experiences in a group.

Conclusion

We wish to concluded by examining the implication of our results and our qualitative methodology for the study of African American men, and for understanding the broader context of redefining masculinity. This article began with the premise that the research literature has, with few exceptions, presented African American fathers as deficient and irresponsible, passive victims of larger social forces. Our research revealed a very different picture. Our study indicate that "African American men" cannot be considered a homogeneous category. The fathers in our sample have creatively and responsibly developed a new pattern of fathering, drawing on traditional Haitian fatherhood, more recent developments in U.S. fathering, and Christian ideology. Our results have illustrated a particular variant of fathering which is a very specific adaptation to Haitian American culture. We assume that the study of a different subculture would reveal yet another specific and creative adaptation.

Our work also has applications to the broader cultural phenomenon of redefining masculinity. The present study indicates that masculine role norms are already in the process of being redefined in this group of Haitian American men. Preliminary date from our larger fathering project suggest that this process is under way in other subcultures as well. We believe that the general social transformation of the masculine role can be studied across subcultures, if viewed through a broad enough theoretical lens. However, we also have found that the particular form the change process takes is highly specific to a local culture. For example, husbands are in the process of sharing some power with their wives in the following middle-class communities that we have studied: Haitian American Christians, white neoconservatives and white politically progressive dual-earner couples. Yet, each subculture begins with specific values and behavior patterns, and then generates unique adaptations and revisions of their existing culture. We have chosen, therefore, to begin by studying local culture, and its indigenous conflicts and resources. Only then can social policy be designed to facilitate the change process by supporting plausible and manageable next steps for each subculture. We call this the "next step" theory of social change.

Finally, we wish to comment on the role of qualitative research in building our "next step" theory. We believe that our findings about Haitian fathers could not have emerged from a more quantitative research design. The senior authors were strangers to the Haitian subculture, and the third author was embedded within it. Therefore none of us was in a position to construct research instruments which had the appropriate balance of cultural relevance and objectivity. This is often the position of researchers approaching previously unstudied, nondominant populations. Consequently, qualitative research is an essential element of these investigations, as a complement to the more traditional quantitative paradigm. Integrating both approaches in the study of human behavior enhances theory building, because good theory must identify trends that are generalizable across groups, and also capture the specific, subjective experience of individuals.

References

Allen, K. R., & Walker, A. J. (1992). A feminist analysis of interviews with elderly mothers and their daughters. In J. E. Gilgun, K. Daly, & G. Handel (Eds.), *Qualitative methods in family research* (pp. 198–214). Newbury Park, CA: Sage.

Bastien, R. (1951). *Le paysan haïtien et sa famille.* (The Haitian peasant and his family). Paris: Editions Karthala.

Biller, H. B. (1968). A note on father absence and masculine development in lower-class Negro and white boys. *Child Development, 40,* 539–546.

Dey, I. (1993). *Qualitative data analysis: A user-friendly guide for social scientists.* New York: Routledge.

Durand, Y. (1980). *Structures familiales en Haïti.* (Family structures in Haiti). *Ethno-psychologie*, 35, 47–51.

Fiorenza, E. (1979). Feminist spirituality, Christian identity, and Catholic vision. In C. P. Christ & J. Plaskow (Eds.), *Womanspirit rising. A feminist reader in religion* (pp. 136–158). New York: Harper & Row.

Geertz, C. (1973). *The interpretation of cultures: Selected essays.* New York: Basic Books.

Geertz. C. (1983). *Local knowledge: Further essays in interpretive anthropology.* New York: Basic Books.

Hossain, Z. E., & Roopnarine, J. L. (1993). Division of household labor and child-care in African American households, *Sex Roles, 29,* 573–583.

Hunter, A.G., & Davis, J. D. (1994). Hidden voices of black men: The meaning, structure, and complexity of manhood. *Journal of Black Studies, 25,* 20–40.

Kiselica, M. (1995). *Multicultural counseling with teen-age fathers: A practical guide.* (Multicultural counseling series, Vol. 6), Newbury Park, CA: Sage.

LaRossa, R. (1988). Fatherhood and social change. F*amily Relations, 37,* 452–457.

Lasry, J. C., & Frédérik, M. (1986). *Structure familiale et pouvoir conjugal dans des familles haïtiennes de Montreal.* (Family structure and marital power among Haitian families in Montreal.) Études Éthniques au Canada, 18, 151–158.

Levant, R. F., & Kopecky, V. (1995). *Masculinity reconstructed: Changing the rules of manhood.* New York: Dutton.

McAdoo, J. A. (1988). Changing perspectives on the role of the African American father. In P. Bronstein & C. P. Cowan (Eds.), *Fatherhood today: Men's changing role in the family* (pp. 79–92). New York: John Wiley & Sons.

McAdoo, J. A. (1993). The role of African American fathers: An ecological perspective. *Journal of Contemporary Human Services, 74,* 28–35.

McClanahan, S. (1986). Family structure and the intergenerational transmission of poverty. *American Journal of Sociology, 90,* 873–901.

McLaughlin, E. (1979). Women in the early Christian movement. In C. P. Christ & J. Plaskow (Eds.), *Womanspirit rising. A feminist reader in religion* (pp. 93–106). New York: Harper & Row.

Miles, M. B. & Huberman, A. M. (1994). *Qualitative data analysis.* Newbury Park, CA: Sage.

Morgan, D. (1988). *Focus groups as qualitative research.* Newbury Park, CA: Sage.

Mott, F. L. (1994). Sons, daughters, and fathers' absence: Differentials in father-leaving probabilities and in-home environments. *Journal of Family Issues, 15,* 97–128.

Moynihan, D. P. (1965). The Negro family: The case for national action. Washington, D.C.: U.S. Department of Labor, Office of Policy, Planning, and Research.

Plaskow, J. (1990). *Standing again at Sinai. Judaism from a feminist perspective.* San Francisco, Harper & Row.

Pleck, J. H. (1991). *The myth of masculinity.* Cambridge, MA: MIT Press.

Pleck, J. H. (1981). Are "family-supportive" employer policies relevant to men? In J. C. Hood (Ed.), *Men, work, and family* (pp. 217–237). Newbury Park, CA: Sage.

Pleck, J. H. (1995). The gender role strain paradigm: An update. In R. F. Levant & W. S. Pollack (Eds.), *A new psychology of men* (pp. 11–32). New York: Basic Books.

Richards, T. J., & Richards, L. (1994). Using computers in qualitative research. In N. Denzin & Y. Lincoln (Eds.), *The handbook of qualitative research* (pp. 445–462). Newbury Park, CA: Sage.

Robinson, B. E. (1988). *Teenage fathers.* Lexington, MA: Lexington Books.

Roopnarine, J. L. & Benetti, S. (1996, March). Caribbean fathers: Marginalized and Distant? Paper presented at the National Center on Fathers and Families, Philadelphia.

Rubin, H. J., & Rubin, I. S. (1995). *Qualitative interviewing: The art of hearing data.* Newbury Park, CA: Sage.

Silverstein, L. (1996). Fathering is a feminist issue. *Psychology of Women Quarterly, 20,* 3–37.

Strauss, A. L. & Corbin, J. (1990). *Basics of qualitative research: Grounded theory procedures and techniques.* Newbury Park, CA: Sage.

Zizi, M. J. (1996). A qualitative study of Haitian Christian men's experience as fathers. Unpublished Psy.D. research project, Ferkauf Graduate School of Psychology, Yeshiva University, Bronx, N.Y.

Auerbach, C., Silverstein, L., & Zizi, M. (1997). The evolving structure of fatherhood among Haitian Americans. *Journal of African American Men, 2,* 59–85.

Appendix C

The Promise Keepers Study

Since the 1960s, U.S. society has been undergoing a process of social evolution. Economic pressures have made it increasingly difficult for most men to fulfull the role of sole provider. The traditional role definitions of fatherhood-as-providing and motherhood-as-nurturing have begun to change. Feminine gender role socialization has been transformed, in that little girls are now socialized to perform roles in the public world of work, as well as the private world of the family. However, masculine gender role socialization has not kept pace with the rapid social changes that families have been experiencing. Although fathers have lost their role as sole provider, cultural ideology, has not yet placed nurturing at the center of the masculine gender role.

In a recent survey of 1,502 women, 48% of married women reported that they provided half or more of a family's income (Lewin, 1995). This new economic power has put pressure on husbands to accept more responsibility for child care and household management. This expanded family role requires them to relinquish some measure of the power and privilege that was formerly associated with the sole provider role. Again, masculine gender role socialization has not yet responded to this demand for men to share power with their wives.

The high divorce rate indicates that these changes in the power relations between men and women stress many marriages. Deprived of their traditional role of sole provider, and pressed to give up male power and privilege, many fathers have become increasingly alienated from their families. This alienation is reflected in the large number of fathers who have little or no emotional connection with their children, within both marital and nonmarital relationships. The high rate of nonpayment of child support by divorced fathers is another indicator of that alienation.

Thus, a central challenge facing contemporary U.S. society is how to encourage responsible fathering behaviors. Our definition of responsible fathering includes; providing economic resources; active involvement in the daily life of children; and parenting in a manner that is emotionally accessible and nurturing, rather than distant and authoritarian. We conceptualize responsible fathering as behavior based on an emotional attachment to a child that is independent of the father's relationship to the child's mother. Thus the dissolution of the mother-father relationship should not preclude continuing emotional attachment and active involvement between father and child.

Two broad social movements are attempting to reconstruct the fathering role in a manner that increases responsible fathering: the pro-feminist men's movement (e.g., Kimmel, 1997; Levant & Pollack, 1995); and the neoconservative men's movement (e.g., Bly, 1990,; McCartney, 1995). The mythopoetic men's movement, the Promise Keepers, and the Million Man March are examples of the neoconservative movement.[1]

The Promise Keepers (PK) is an evangelical Christian organization founded by the former head football coach of the University of Colorado, Bill McCartney. McCartney's epiphany occurred when his unwed teenage daughter gave birth to a child fathered by one of the players on his football team. He decided to leave Catholicism, and ultimately his high-profile job, in order to begin a movement of "men coming together in huge numbers in the name of Jesus, worshiping and celebrating their faith together . . . [and] proclaiming their love to Christ and their commitment to their families" (McCartney, 1995, p. 286).

McCartney's (1995) vision for PK is a "ministry of reconciliation," in which men give up the practice of "empty promises" (p. 286). McCartney asserted that the majority of men, himself included, have focused too intensely on their work lives, and have given up responsibility as leader of the family. The seven promises of a Promise Keeper (Dobson, 1994) include: honoring Jesus, pursuing vital relationships with other men, and building a strong marriage and family.

In contrast to pro-feminist men's groups, neoconservative groups have been effective in attracting the participation of large numbers (rallies of 50,000 to 200,000) of men. However, the fundamentalist nature of neoconservative ideology is a matter of concern to feminist men and women, and to the gay/lesbian community. Neoconservative ideology generally promotes a hierarchical power relationship of male dominance over women in families. It defines parenting roles as linked to biological differences between men and women. In addition, when it is combined with religious fundamentalism, it condemns homosexuality. The growing popularity of these movements is even more alarming in light of recent reports that neoconservative groups, like the Promise Keepers, have received extensive funding from the political Right (Conason, Ross, & Cokorinos, 1996).

Despite these negative characteristics, each of these neoconservative men's movements also advocates some aspects of responsible fathering, as we have defined it. The mixed messages embedded within neoconservative ideology thus place us, as feminist theorists, in a difficult position. We approach fathering from a feminist perspective that values active fathering without subordinating mothers or minimizing their importance. We believe that nurturing and caretaking are activities that are as central to responsible fatherhood as to motherhood. Our theoretical model assumes that positive father involvement can exist within many different family forms, including mother-headed, gay/lesbian, and step-parenting families. Thus, we reject the philosophy of male dominance, anti-gay/lesbian bias; and the biologically linked definition of complementary parenting roles. On the other hand, we support the elements of neoconservative ideology which encourage responsible, nurturing fathering behaviors.

We began our study from a theoretical perspective that nurturing fathering had the potential to transform traditional masculine gender role socialization. Thus, we assumed that the process of redefining fathering would create opportunities for reconstructing patriarchy. We speculated that, by supporting nurturing fathering behaviors, these neoconservative movements could potentially contribute to feminist goals.

We also believed that the aims of the political leadership of these neo-conservative movements must be distinguished from the goals of the grass-roots membership. As Frank Rich (1996, p. A21) has observed about members of the Promise Keepers, the individual men "seem more motivated by a Robert Blysesque hunger to overcome macho inhibitions and reconnect with God, than by any desire to enlist is a political army." Most of the information reported about the Promise Keepers has been gleaned through reading their "official" texts (McCartney, 1995), or from attending evangelical meetings which are aimed at inspiring hundreds of thousands of men. These sources present ideological and political positions which may not be shared by the grassroots membership.

Our goal in the current research project was to listen to the subjective experiences of a group of Promise Keepers, and to explore the ways in which becoming a member of the Promise Keepers had affected the men's fathering behaviors. In this article, we present a qualitative research study of one group of Promise Keeper fathers. We discuss these research findings in terms of our theoretical model of the evolution of fatherhood identities. We offer suggestions of ways in which the pro-feminist men's movement might become more effective in encouraging men to construct a more progressive fatherhood role.

Methodology

Procedure

The current study was part of a larger research project studying fatherhood identities from many different subcultures within the United States. Our research approach involved the use of a qualitative, hypothesis-generating paradigm. To date, we have completed data collection on groups of Haitian Christian fathers; Latino fathers; gay fathers; Orthodox Jewish fathers, Greek Orthodox fathers; and the current group of Promise Keeper fathers. Each sample contained from 20 to 24 fathers who volunteered to participate in the project. Data on the Haitian fathers has been previously published (Auerbach, Silverstein, Zizi, 1997). The Promise Keepers sample is the second data set to be fully analyzed and published.

We collected data in focus groups, which are semi-structured group interviews, in which a moderator takes the group members through a

Table C.1
Focus Group Questions

1. What was the first time you thought about being a father, and what did you think it would be like?
2. What is your relationship with your father, and how has it affected your fathering?
3. How did you and your wife go through the process of deciding to have a child?
4. What is being a father like? How did it change your sense of who you are, and what your life is about?
5. What are you most proud of, and what do you most regret?
6. How has being a father affected your relationship with your parents and siblings?
7. How has the Promise Keepers influenced your attitudes toward fathering?

narrative account of their fathering experience (Morgan, 1998). The groups were conducted by a graduate student moderator under our supervision. Each student had a particular interest in the culture that she or he studied, and often was a member of it. Each study used four or five focus groups.

Each focus group was structured around six open-ended questions (see Table C.1). Some of the questions yielded responses more relevant to the concerns of this article than others, and consequently are over-represented in the current data analysis. The group interviews were videotaped and transcribed. The transcripts constituted the material for qualitative data analysis.

Our data analysis procedure used a grounded theory methodology (Strauss & Corbin, 1990) which has evolved over the course of the project (see Auerbach et al., 1997) for a more detailed description of the research methodology. It involved a coding procedure with three levels. The first level, the text-based category, coded words and phrases used regularly and repeatedly throughout the text. The second level, the sensitizing concept, coded culturally specific ideas and understandings implicit in the text-based categories. The third and highest level, the theoretical construct, reflected our organization of the sensitizing concepts into a theoretical framework. Each level subsumed the level below it. That is, each sensitizing concept is a cluster of text-based categories, and each theoretical construct is a cluster of sensitizing concepts (see Table C.3). Each transcript was coded by four coders: the two senior authors, and two graduate students.

In their discussion of how qualitative research should be used to generate theory, Strauss and Corbin (1997) recommended that a theoretical concept derived from an initial data set should be refined using subsequent data sets. They call this process *theoretical sampling,* that is, sampling on the basis of concepts that have "proven theoretical relevance to the evolving theory" (p.176). We have followed this procedure.

The two senior authors derived three theoretical constructs about fatherhood identities from their analysis of data in the earlier study of Haitian fathers (see Auerbach et al., 1997): bicultural gender role strain; constructing a more gratifying definition of fathering; facilitating ideology. The two senior authors tried to code the Promise Keeper data independently of those earlier theoretical constructs, although the framework undoubtedly had some impact on their thinking. The two junior authors had not participated in the prior study of Haitian Christian fathers, and thus were unfamiliar with the theoretical framework.

As we will describe below, the current data set refined our theoretical framework in several ways. Two of the prior constructs were more precisely defined, and data emerged reflecting a fourth theoretical construct. We also took the procedure to another level, in that we have used the theoretical constructs to develop a theory about how men change to become more involved fathers.

As suggested by Rubin & Rubin (1995), we have incorporated many safeguards to assure the qualitative equivalents of reliability and validity. We aim for a procedure which is *transparent* (another investigator can know and check what we have done); *communicable* (the categories make sense to both the participants themselves, and to other investigators who want to use them); and *coherent* (the categories are simultaneously internally consistent, and reflect both individual differences and genuine inconsistencies in the culture).

Research Participants

The group moderator was a white, female graduate student whose religious beliefs made her sympathetic to the beliefs of the Promise Keepers. A friend of the moderator's was a member of the Promise Keepers who recruited participants for the first three groups. For the fourth group, the moderator contacted the National Center for Fathering in Kansas City through the Internet. The center supplied the names of two fathers in the metropolitan NYC area, who recruited participants for the fourth group.

Four focus groups were conducted ranging from three to seven fathers in each group. In addition to the standard questions of the research project, the interviewer asked the men about their beliefs as Promise Keepers, and the influence of the Promise Keepers on their fathering behaviors.

The group included 22 men ranging in age from their late twenties to their early sixties (27 to 61, X = 43). Two of the men were African American. The other 20 were white. All of the white men were Euroamerican, except for one who was American. The men all came from New Jersey, and had incomes ranging from $25,000 to $200,000 (X = $66,000). All of the men except one were married. They had between one and four children (X = 2), ranging in age from 7 months to 35 years. All of the men in the sample attended Promise Keeper meetings on a weekly basis. (See Table C.2)

Results

Table C.2

A Frequency Distribution of the Participant by Age, Income, Number of Children

Category	*n*	(%)
Age		
27–40	9	(41)
41–49	8	(36)
51–90	5	(23)
Income (in $1000)		
0–15	1	(05)
16–30	2	(09)
31–50	9	(41)
51–90	6	(27)
91–200	4	(18)
Number of Children		
1	4	(18)
2	9	(41)
3	7	(32)
4	2	(09)

N = 22.

Table C.3

Theoretical Constructs, Sensitizing Concepts, and Text-Base Categories

I. Gender role strain; Failure of traditional masculine role norms.	
A. Unhappy early experience with their father.	73%
1. My father was never really around.	
2. I know how *not* to be a father.	
B. Struggling with their own fathering.	67%
3. Anxiety about fathering.	
4. Feeling unprepared for fatherhood.	
C. Relying on the traditional masculine role.	77%
5. A man has to be strong.	
6. Providing is everything.	
II. Ideology: A new husband/father paradigm.	
D. Your family as the most important part of your life.	100%
8. Relationships are the most important thing.	
9. Alternatives to anger.	
E. Men must accept the leadership role.	
10. Men are spiritual leaders of their families.	
11. You can only lead by serving.	
12. Men and women: different but equal.	
III. Social supports: A brotherhood of men.	
F. Male support	100%
13. PK makes you realize you are not alone.	
14. PK helps you acknowledge your vulnerabilities.	
IV. Personal gratification: Connecting to God and family.	
G. Doing God's Work.	41%
15. Your family is a gift from God.	
H. PK reconnects you to family.	100%
16. Improved relationship with wife.	
17. Improved relationship with extended family.	

N = 22. In the original data analysis, the percentages were calculated for each text-based category. However, in the current paper, our interpretation is at the sensitizing concept level. Therefore, the percentages here are given for the sensitizing concepts, and reflect the proportion of the sample that expressed a comment in any of the text-based categories which are grouped under a particular sensitizing concept.

Sensitizing Concepts and Text-Driven Categories

UNHAPPY EARLY EXPERIENCES WITH THEIR FATHERS

Although a minority of the men in this sample reported having positive relationships with their father (N = 6; 27%), the majority of men (N = 16; 73%) had either negative or distant relationship with their own fathers. About half of the men had good alternate role models, including their mother (13%)., whereas the others felt they had no positive models at all.

My Father Was Never Really Around

> I lost my father early on {to suicide}, so I did not have a stable family to think about. (El, Group 2)

> I didn't know my father. I met him once. (J1, Group 1)

> My mother and father got divorced when I was about five years old, so my father was never really around that much. (C1, Group 2)

I Know How Not to Be a Father

> I do the opposite of what my dad did, I figure, that must be right. (J2, Group 4)

> I feel he has had a negative effect on my own fathering. (S, Group 3)

> [I didn't see much of my father,] This made me realize, "spend as much time with them as possible." (J3, Group 1)

STRUGGLING WITH THEIR OWN FATHERING

Given their lack of positive relationships with their own fathers, the majority of men (67%) reported feeling unprepared to assume a fathering role, and uncertain about manhood in general. Some used their fathers as negative role models, doing the opposite of what their fathers had done. They also had the sense that their wives somehow knew how to be mothers whereas, they had not been taught to think of themselves as responsible parents.

Anxiety about Fathering

I really got kind of scared about being a father. (F, Group1)

I didn't want to become a father because I really didn't have a role model. (E1, Group 2)

Feeling Unprepared for Fatherhood

After we had our first child, I realized that I probably wasn't prepared to be a father. (C2, Group 4)

I was striving to understand what manhood was. In the early days, I thought, "there's no manual that tells you how to be a good husband, a good father." (Group 1, B)

Men are never raised to be fathers, but women are raised to be mothers. (E2, Group 3)

RELYING ON THE TRADITIONAL MASCULINE ROLE

Without a "fathering manual," almost 80% (77%) of the men constructed a fathering identity based on traditional masculine norms. David and Brannon (1976) define the traditional masculine role as including an emphasis on: physical toughness and emotional stoicism, achievement; aggression, avoidance of all things feminine, and homophobia.

A Man Has to Be Strong

You're the big strong hero, and you can't break down, you can't let things out. (M1, Group 3)

The message I got when I was growing up was that you were supposed to be all-knowing. (A, Group 1)

Providing Is Everything

I didn't really think much about parenting, I thought about what I was going to do for my occupation. (T, Group 1)

> Shortly after my wife delivered, I realized there was an obligation to provide. (S, Group 3)

Building a Wall

> I started building a wall up, because every decision that was made I felt I could make on my own. Before I knew it, I had isolated myself. (T, Group 1)

> It's like facing the barrel of a shot gun—for most men to really open their hearts . . . revealing who they are and the things that we fear. (E1, Group 2)

YOUR FAMILY IS THE MOST IMPORTANT PART OF YOUR LIFE

The following quotes indicate the contrast between the way that the men constructed their fathering identities before and after their involvement with the Promise Keeper movement. They describe how PK helped them to become more responsive to their families. They used scripture to shift their emphasis from a definition of fathering-as providing, to a more nurturing version of fathering. They also stated that they have learned how to listen to, rather than lecture, their wives and children. Finding alternatives to angry confrontation was another skill they felt they had learned from their weekly Promise Keeper meetings. They give example of learning to listen to their acting-out adolescent daughter, rather than responding automatically with anger; and presenting a sensitive, rather than angry role model for their sons. By identifying with Jesus as a loving God, they were able to relinquish their more remote emotional stance.

Relationships Are the Most Important Thing

> With my older daughter, I never had the time to sit and talk. Through PK, through the Bible, I learned that the Lord is our heavenly father, and we have to look at our children the same way that He looks at us. (M1, Group 3)

PK gave me a bolder look about the real responsibility of fathering. It is not only providing physically, you must provide emotional nourishment. (E1, Group 3)

You for that someday it's all going to over, and putting in extra time at the office may not be as important as being home with your kids. (R, Group 1)

Alternatives to Anger

PK is teaching me to learn how to forgive and work through the anger. (F, Group 1)

I need to be sensitive to my son. How else will he learn to be sensitive to others? (J2, Group 4)

My life turned around 100% just by listening to my kids. (M1, Group 3)

MEN MUST ACCEPT THE LEADERSHIP ROLE

In return for becoming more emotionally available, and less explicitly domineering, Promise Keeper ideology proposed that fathers are essential to their children's development, and that husbands are the leaders of the family. This allowed the men to retain a dominant status viz a viz their wives.

However, the men stated that PK teaching explicitly rejected an abuse of power, by stipulating that leadership requires modeling responsibility. One must live that responsible role, not simply give lip service to it.

Men Are the Spiritual Leaders of Their Families

PK says a family has to have a father to raise the children. (D, Group 4)

PK is teaching us to be the spiritual leaders of our house, not the king of castle. (M1, Group 3)

The issues of leadership, hierarchy, and power were complex, from both a behavioral and an ideological perspective. In order to become more responsible husbands and fathers, PK ideology exhorted the men to give up some aspects of male privilege and power. They must listen to their wives, share household tasks and childcare, and spend less time at work and in leisure time activities outside the family. However, PK also reassured them that they were not giving up power and privilege. Thus the paradoxical message that message that "one must lead by serving."

You Can Only Lead by Serving

> Being a father is a serving job, not a ruling job. It's not about ordering people around the house and telling them what to do. It's about being the first to care about the needs of the rest of the members of your family. (J1, Group7)

> Leader does not mean being the boss. Leaders are men who lead by example. (C1, Group 6)

> Christ is the head of the Church, but he was willing to sacrifice His life for eternity. In the same way, the husband is head of the family. (E1, Group 3)

Men and Woman: Different but Equal

> The Scriptures say women are just as important as men. We are co-equal, but different. (S, Group 3)

> My wife is very meek, she's very submissive. Now I allow her to take two steps forward, and I take two steps back. (T, Group 1)

> God created us to be complementary. Different is not necessarily bad. (J1, Group 1)

MALE SUPPORT

As the men struggled to redefine themselves in terms of becoming a more emotionally responsive father and husband, 100% of the men reported that the weekly Promise Keepers meetings provided them with a supportive setting which helped them manage their anxiety. They felt reassured that they were not struggling with these issues alone, Promise Keepers gave the men a support group of Christian men within which "being manly" included being vulnerable.

PK Makes You Feel You Are Not Alone

Men begin to talk, and you learn that you are not alone . . . you get a chance to hear what it is that makes up manhood from men who have actually worked at it. (J1, Group 1)

I just feel sorry for those men who try to do it on their own. (P, Group 4)

You can call one another, speak with another brother, find out if these brothers are going through much the same thing. (E1, Group 2)

PK Helps You Acknowledge Your Vulnerabilities

I realize I don't have to hold emotions. (E1, Group 2)

One man giving another man permission to be vulnerable. (A, Group 1)

PK teaches you how to get through your problems. How to have a softness of heart . . . that you have to cry, you have to break down as a man. (M1, Group 3)

DOING GOD'S WORK

Finally, about 40% of the men stated that being a good father, as PK defined it, provided them with a sense of profound connection to God. Thus changes in their behaviors provided personal gratification at a profound level. Virtually all of the men described their pleasure at being emotionally reconnected to their wives and children. About half also reported that fathering generated a sense of common purpose with their parents and siblings.

Your Family Is a Gift from God

They are a gift from God to you, and you treat them as such. (E2, Group 3)

I do things the way the Lord wants them. (C1, Group 2)

When I took our kids to PK, I had never felt closer to my son than when I saw him being enlightened. (C2, Group 4)

PK RECONNECTS YOU TO FAMILY

Improved Relationship with Wife

> Before PK, I made all the decision. PK has given me values—to see what my wife says about something. When a decision has to be made, we sit down and pray. (T, Group 1)

> It changed me, I'm a better husband. I care about my wife more. I listen to her more. (M2, Group 2)

> It made me less selfish with my wife. My background was—you eat dinner and the men go in the living room and watch TV, and the women bring in the ice cream. Now you do things together. (J2, Group 4)

Improves Relationship with Extended Family

> PK has taken the sharpness away from my personality. My family is more accessible to me now. (T, Group 1)

> It's helped me realize just how difficult fathering is . . . both my brothers are married and we share the common responsibility of fathering. (S, Group 3)

Theoretical Constructs

Our data analysis in the Haitian fathers study (Auerbach et al., 1997) generated three theoretical constructs: bicultural gender role strain; a facilitating ideology, and a personally gratifying definition of fatherhood. We have refined and modified these constructs based on data from the current study. In addition, a fourth construct emerged, social supports in the form of relationships with others which help bind anxiety about change. The results of the current study are discussed in terms of these four theoretical constructs (see Table C.3).

Gender Role Strain: The Failure of Traditional Masculine Role Norms

The Promise Keeper fathers entered marriage feeling unprepared to become a husband/father. As one man said "There's no manual . . . no book

Table C.4
Comparing Fatherhood Ideologies

Role Definition	Description
Traditional	1. Father as patriarch. 2. Biologically linked complementary role. 3. Emotional distance, lack of active involvement. 4. Defined by nuclear family structure.
Neoconservative	1. Father as spiritual leader. 2. Biologically linked complementary roles. 3. Emotionally connected, active involvement. 4. Defined by nuclear family structure.
Progressive	1. Power-sharing. 2. Role-sharing. 3. Emotionally connected, active involvement. 4. Can exist within diverse family structures

on what you need to do to be a good husband, to be a good father" (J1, Group 1). Many of the men had not known their own fathers, or had unsatisfying relationships with them.

Feeling lost and unprepared for their new role, they relied on traditional masculinity ideology to suggest how they should behave. However, the traditional fathering role (see Table C.4), with its emphasis on providing and its lack of emotional connectedness, was unsatisfying to the men, their wives, and children. Thus, although the men conformed to traditional role norms, they could not make themselves or their families happy. Their wives were critical of their preoccupation with work, and their unwillingness to participate in spiritual activities. Their children felt emotionally alienated from them.

Another aspect of the gender role strain that the men were feeling was a conflict between authoritarianism and accessibility. The traditional masculine role defines men as powerful providers/protectors. However, this dominant stance further inhibited their inability to listen. Yet the men could not comfortably share power and acknowledge their vulnerabilities, because this would contradict traditional masculine role norms.

Facilitating Ideology: A New Husband/Father Paradigm

The Promise Keeper ideology provided a means for the men to resolve this role strain, and construct a more satisfying husband/father role. The Promise Keeper fathers used Christian doctrine to change some of the problematic aspects of the traditional masculine role norms. These men used Jesus as a role model. Jesus was a warm and loving deity who had an intensely personal relationship with his followers. This model encouraged the fathers to give up their distant, authoritarian stance, and to shift their priority from being a good provider, to focusing on having personal relationships with their children.

We speculate that traditional masculine role norms are so powerful, that some men only feel comfortable violating them "on higher authority." Jesus and the Bible provided that higher authority.

Learning to listen, and becoming more involved in childcare required relinquishing some aspects of male power and privilege. However, the Promise Keepers maintained symbolic power and sense of importance by becoming the "spiritual head" of the family. Yet this dominance status was softened, again using Jesus as a role mode. Because the leadership role was defined as "leading by serving." Although a wife and children are required to "submit" to the husband's leadership, leading-by-serving is defined in terms of responsibility and sacrifice. Like Jesus, a father is supposed to put the needs of the family above his own. Thus, PK ideology provides a *tromp l'oeil* face-saving way for men to share power by being godlike. From their perspective, the their investment in paid work in order to spend more time with their children. We believe that, compared to their behavior prior to joining the Promise Keepers do not believe that they devalue women. Their perspective is that they define men and women as different, but co-equal.

Social Supports: A Brotherhood of Men

The men also spoke about the importance of meeting in groups with other Promise Keeper men. From our perspective, these meetings, like the consciousness raising groups of the early feminist movement, were helpful in managing the anxiety that inevitable accompanies role change. Despite the rhetoric, we believe that these men are in the process of transforming their behaviors to conform to a more progressive version of the fathering role.

These men are making choices to limit their investment in paid work in order to spend more time with their children. We believe that, compared to their behavior prior to joining the Promise Keepers, they are behaving more respectfully toward their wives, assuming more responsibility for childcare, and decreasing the emotional distance between themselves and their children.

These new behaviors on the part of men are not yet supported by a change in cultural gender ideology or widespread social policy supports. Pleck (1993) has shown that U.S. workplace policies are not supportive of men limiting their commitment to work in order to be more involved with their children. Thus, we speculate that the changes these men were making probably caused them some degree of anxiety. The Promise Keepers organization helped their members cope with this change process by providing weekly support groups where the men could receive psychological support *from other men.* This psychological support reassured the men that they were not alone in their struggle, and that their behavior changes did not mean that they were not "real men."

Personal Gratification: Reconnecting to God and to Family

Their new behaviors provided the men with a sense of being close to God. This experience of spiritual well-being further reinforced their new definition of the husband/father role. They also reported feeling much more appreciated by their wives and children. The sense of closeness to their families contrasted with the emotional distance and alienation that the men had described prior to their entrance into the Promise Keeper community. Thus, the sense of emotional connectedness was a powerful reward which enhanced the change process.

Some men also reported that their new sense of themselves as responsible husband/fathers has made them feel closer to their families of origin. Family systems theory (Kerr & Bowen, 1988) has proposed that a sense of connectedness to extended family contributes to psychological health by decreasing chronic anxiety. Thus, this positive linkage with extended family is another powerful reinforcement for continued behavior change.

The Next Step Theory of Social Change

This section illustrates how we have organized the four theoretical constructs into a broad theoretical framework that we have called "The Next Step Theory of Social Change." As both clinicians and researchers,we believe that interventions must be multisystemic in order to be effective. They must operate at the level of the individual; the social groups; and the larger culture. It is the complex interplay between these systemic levels which determines whether the intervention will be successful.

The first component of our theory, gender role strain, represents an intrapsychic experience of discomfort. In general, the men did not have a good relationship with their own fathers, and felt anxious about their ability to be good fathers ("Unhappy early experiences with their own fathers"; "Struggling with their own fathering"). They tried to be the best kind of father they know how to be, by being good providers and strong, emotionally stoic men ("Relying on traditional masculine role norms"). However, these behaviors left them feeling emotionally isolated from their wives and children. This internal experience of gender role strain provided the motivation for change.

However, two external supports were necessary to transform this motivation into action: a facilitating cultural ideology which prescribed new behaviors, and a system of social relationships that helped the men manage the anxiety associated with change. The PK ideology urged the men to shift their priority from providing financial resources to spending more time with their families ("Your family as the most important part of your life"). It also encouraged them to give up their authoritarian and emotionally distant stance. The ideology also reassured them that, although they were giving up some of the power associated with an authoritarian stance, they were still the leader of the family ("Men must accept the leadership role").

Similarly, PK provided weekly meetings of other Christian men who talked about struggling with the issue of sharing responsibility and becoming more emotionally accessible ("Male support"). These meetings reassured them that they were not the only ones feeling anxious about change. The new role norms and the social support system that reinforced them helped the men construct a new fathering identity which was more personally gratifying ("Doing God's work," "PK connects you to family").

Figure C.1
The Next Step Theory of Social Change

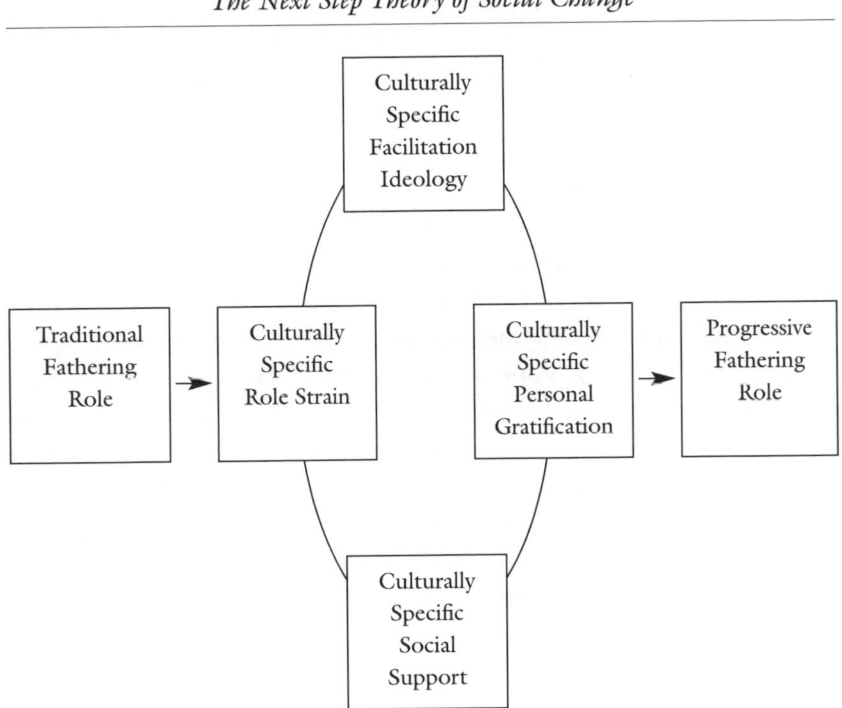

They felt that they were conforming to a spiritual mandate. In addition, they felt more emotionally connected to their wives and extended family. This sense of personal gratification then became another component that reinforced their new behaviors.

We hypothesize that these four components of the change process interact in a nonlinear, circular fashion (see Fig. C.1). We also believe that each of these factors is culturally specific. For example, a facilitating ideology must reflect the values of the subculture of the men being studied. In the current study and in our previous study of Haitian Christian men (Auerbach et al., 1997), the men were members of a fundamentalist religious subculture. Thus, the facilitating ideologies were based on Biblical ideas. In another study of gay fathers (Quartironi, 1995), the facilitating ideology was based on the gay civil rights movement. In our sample of dual-earner, middle-class suburban fathers, the ideology was based on attitudes about fairness in dual provider couples (Weinberg, 1997).

The sources of social support are also culturally specific. In our Haitian and Promise Keeper groups, only men who shared their religious fundamentalist ideology could have provided the emotional support the fathers needed in order to change. In our gay fathers groups, *only* people, both gay and nongay, who supported gay men as parents could provide support to those fathers.

Similarly, D'Andrade (1992), a cognitive anthropologist, has proposed that gratification results from the achievement of goals, and that an individual's goals are determined by cultural values. Our research findings also have suggested that the personal gratification that the fathers experienced was culturally specific. The men felt good about themselves only if they were conforming to the values of their specific ideology. For example, in the religious fundamentalist subcultures of Haitian Christian fathers and Promise Keeper fathers, feeling closer to God was an important part of the personal gratification the men felt. In contrast, for our sample of dual earner, middle-class, suburban fathers, religious feelings, were not part of their sense of gratification. Rather, they felt good about being involved fathers because sharing the responsibility for childcare with their working wives conformed to their sense of fairness.

Our research has suggested that there are many subcultures of fatherhood, each with its specific version of gender role strain, each requiring a culturally specific ideology and social support system; and each generating a sense of personal gratification which is based on specific cultural values.

Discussion

Limitation of the Study

Before turning to the broader implications of the study, it is important to acknowledge its limitations. The participants were volunteers, and therefore, may not be representative of Promise Keeper fathers in general. The meaning and importance of family, and their willingness to divulge personal information, may be greater among these participants than in Promise keepers as a whole. In addition, the number of stress factors in the lives of fathers who refused or who were not asked to participate may be greater than in the participants' lives.

The study also suffers from the limitations of all self-report studies in that the participants' responses may have been influenced by social desirability. The focus group format may have exacerbated this problem. The men may have felt pressure to conform to the attitudes expressed by other members of the group. Some of the focus groups were composed of men who knew each other. Thus, the men did not have the confidentiality that would have been provided if the groups had been composed of strangers. The data thus may reflect more consensus than actually exists among Promise Keeper members.

The responses were also structured by the interview questions. If the groups had been more open-ended, different kinds of data may have emerged. The presence of a female moderator who was not a member of the Promise Keeper community may also have influenced the content of the men's responses. Subsequent studies of Promise Keepers and their wives are needed to test the accuracy of the findings, and their generalizability to other Promise Keeper members.

Implications of the Study: The Appeal of the Neoconservative Movement

In addition to understanding the experience of this particular group of Promise Keeper fathers, another goal of the current study was to understand how the neoconservative movement has succeeded in attracting the participation of large numbers of men. Especially since the more progressive pro-feminist men's movement has not. Our next step theory suggests that the Promise Keepers movement provides men with two components that are essential to the change process: a facilitating ideology, and a social support system.

The Promise Keeper ideology facilitates change by encouraging men to relinquish the provider role as the centerpiece of their fathering identity, and to embrace a more nurturing role. However, in addition to prescribing change, the PK ideology *maintains* aspects of the traditional fathering role by preserving a leadership role for men in the family. By redefining the father as spiritual leader, rather than patriarch, the father maintains power and status. Similarly, the concept of complementary parenting roles reinforces the more traditional role definitions of mother-nurturer and father provider. This focus on complementary roles also emphasizes the importance of the traditional nuclear family. This family structure, in contrast to mother-headed or gay father-headed families, further enhances the centrality of heterosexual men. Thus PK ideology represents a combination of traditional and progressive values. It both facilitates change and maintains the status quo.

The pro-feminist men's ideology, in contrast, does not preserve any aspects of the traditional fathering role. Rather, the progressive fathering role asks men to relinquish *all* aspects of male power and privilege, and to adopt an egalitarian form of decision-making. Similarly, men are not reassured about their distinctive role in family life. Rather, mothers and fathers are defined as interchangeable; and all family forms are considered viable.

Thus progressive ideology has challenged the concept that fathering is a unique role, and that men are essential to positive outcomes for children. This ideology has also rejected the idea that the traditional nuclear family is the best form of family life. Positive child outcomes are seen as possible within many diverse family structures, including lesbian and gay families. Many men have understood this message as the equivalent of declaring (heterosexual) men irrelevant (Blankenhorn, 1995; Popenoe, 1996). Thus progressive fathering ideology, rather than helping men *contain* anxiety, may actually generate *more* anxiety in many men.

Another key aspect of the Promise Keepers movement that supports the change process is the system of social supports, weekly group meetings. These meetings help bind the men's anxiety by assuring them that they are not alone in their struggle with the demands of the husband/father role. They hear other men talk about behaving in nontraditional ways, such as sharing housework, or listening to rather than lecturing their children. We believe that this sense of solidarity in the process of giving up male power and privilege is enormously reassuring. The men realize that they can violate some traditional masculine role norms, and still remain "real men."

It may be that most people need this type of group support when change is focused in the direction of revising traditional social norms. The transformation of the traditional feminine role required the social support of feminist consciousness raising groups in the 1970s. Our research suggests that men need to belong to a community of men who share the same values and validate new, nontraditional behaviors. The progressive men's movement has not yet developed an equivalent system of men's support

Table C.5
Appeal of the Neoconservative Movement

1. Addresses men's internal experience.
   a. Feelings of inadequacy are lessened through identification with God.
   b. Symbolic power and privilege are maintained through the position of "spiritual head" of the family.
   c. Emotional isolation is decreased because relationships are now defined as central to manhood.
2. Ideology legitimates power sharing and role sharing.
   a. Identification with Jesus as God maintains a sense of power.
   b. Since Jesus sacrificed his life for humanity, sacrifice and serving are placed at the center of men's family role.
3. Social support system (church congregation, men's groups).
   a. Men are no longer isolated from other men.
   b. Men are encouraged to acknowledge their vulnerability.
4. Improved relationships.
   a. Men are no longer on the emotional periphery of family life.
   b. Men's need for closeness is gratified.
   c. Men feel connected to their families of origin.

groups to help with the complex task of constructing a more progressive husband/father role.

Neoconservative social commentator social commentators have been successful in generating a national debate about fatherhood (e.g., Blankenhorn, 1995; Popenoe, 1996). Given the current societal concern about responsible fathering, it might be the right historical moment to organize fathering groups within schools, religious institutions, and the workplace to support men as they struggle to construct a more expanded family role. If President Clinton's daycare initiative is implemented, day care centers may be a useful setting for large numbers of men to meet discuss their fatherhood experiences.

Table C.5 outlines how the neoconservative movement conforms to our next step theory of social change. The movement recognizes men's intrapsychic distress (gender role strain); provides a facilitating ideology that prescribes new role behaviors, and supplies a system of weekly support groups where men can talk about their struggles with other men. The men have been able to make changes in their husband/father behaviors that have generated an internal sense of spiritual fulfillment, and interpersonal rewards which further reinforced their behavioral changes.

Our "Next Step Theory" proposes that behavior change proceeds in increments that are small enough, and culturally consistent enough, to generate manageable anxiety. Vygotsky (1978) defined effective teaching as working within a learner's zone of "proximal development." The progressive men's movement may require traditional men to take too many steps, too quickly. It may be that for most men, feminist power-sharing and gay affirmative ideology are outside of their "zone of proximal development." Similarly, until very recently, most women have been economically dependent on men, and have derived whatever power and status they had from the men in their lives (father and husband). Most adult women have been socialized to defer to men. Thus, feminist power-sharing ideology and gay affirmative attitudes may be outside of the "zone of proximal development" for many women as well. In our experience, change occurs only when a person can comfortably take the "next" step.

Conclusion

In addition to acknowledging that PK ideology has helped men change in the direction of a more nurturing, responsible fathering role, it is also important to underline that the ideology also limits progressive change. Fundamentalist religious ideology is exclusive, rather than inclusive. This ideology insists that the heterosexual nuclear family is the only acceptable version of family life, rejecting homosexual lifestyles and nontraditional family structures. Similarly, these values support a male power hierarchy within families. This power structure reinforces traditional authoritarian relationships between men and their wives and children.

In response to the homophobia and male dominance implicit in their ideology. Kimmel (1997) has expressed the distrust that the progressive men's movement and feminists have toward the Promise Keepers. He characterized PK as a "kinder, gentler patriarchy" (p. 48). Kimmel has cited the statements of many national leaders, such as the Reverend Ed Cole, who stated that "God's revelation came through man, not woman," as evidence that the movement is based on an ideology of male supremacy (Kimmel, 1997, p. 48).

We agree that protecting male power is a central goal of the leaders of the Promise Keepers movement. Yet, we believe that the changes that the individual men in this study have made in the direction of progressive fathering should be acknowledged. As feminist theorists, we were predisposed to feel very negatively toward these fathers. However, we listened to them describe their struggle to be more actively involved with their children, to be more respectful of their wives, and to share in household responsibilities. We became convinced that the Promise Keeper movement was helping them transform their fathering role from a more emotionally distant provider model, to a more emotionally connected, role-sharing model. Therefore, we have adopted a "both/and" position; rejecting the male dominance and heterocentrism implicit with the *ideology*; while supporting the efforts of *individual men* to become more emotionally accessible and actively involved fathers.

Before beginning our fathering research, we had hoped that, if men became more emotionally connected nurturing fathers, this would inevitably lead to transforming masculinity ideology, and eventually, to dismantling patriarchy. However, after studying several groups of fathers, we now believe that emotionally accessible, nurturing fathering is necessary, but not sufficient, for transforming traditional masculinity. Two additional components are necessary: a commitment to power sharing rather than male dominance; and a respect for individual differences, including homosexuality.

We now believe that more nurturing fathering does not lead inevitably to the achievement of feminist foals, at least not within a single generation. However, it may be that the lived experience of having a more emotionally connected, less authoritarian father may lead the daughter of these PK fathers to marry even more progressive men. Similarly, the sons of these PK fathers may continue to develop a more progressive masculine identity. In this way, the PK movement may contribute to the evolution of masculinity ideology in a pro-feminist direction. Therefore, our answer to the question. "Do Promise Keepers dream of feminist sheep?" is "Perhaps, but they don't (yet) remember their dreams."

Notes

The coded data from the current study were organized by Loretta Grieco, and submitted as a Psy.D. research project in partial fulfillment of her doctoral degree (Grieco, 1996). For the purposes of the current article, the data were reanalyzed and reorganized by the two senior authors.

1. Some social commentators have objected to grouping the mythopoetic men's movement with other neoconservative groups (e.g., Kimmel, 1998). As we understand this argument, pro-feminist social commentators have acknowledged that Bly's (1990) ideology is essentialist and misogynist, a "new hegemonic masculinity" (Messner, 1995, p. 104). However, they see two aspects of the mythopeotic movement as redeeming; it provides an opportunity for men to come together to talk about their feelings, and the movement is diverse enough to include some leaders who have moved in a more progressive direction than Bly's original ideological stance.

We agree with these two assessments of the mythopoetic men's movement. However, we will make a similar argument about the Promise Keepers. We believe that the weekly PK meetings provide a forum for men to talk about their vulnerabilities with other men. Similarly, we think that the ideology of the leaders is more reactionary than the behavior of the individual men in our study. Thus we see the Promise Keepers and the mythopoetic movements as more similar than different. We believe that Kimmel's characterization of some aspects of the mythopoetic movement (1997, p. 38) as "a progressive whisper within a reactive structure," could also be applied to the men in the Promise Keeper's movement.

References

Auerbach, C., Silverstein, L., & Zizi, M. (1997). The evolving structure of fatherhood: A qualitative study of Haitian American fathers. *Journal of African American Men, 2,* 59–85.

Blankenhorn, D. (1995). *Fatherless America: Confronting our most urgent social problem.* New York: Basic Books.

Bly, R. (1990). *Iron John.* New York: Addison-Wesley.

Conason, J., Ross, A., & Cokorinos, L. (1996, October 7). The Promise Keepers are coming: The third wave of the religious right. *The Nation,* pp. 11–19.

D'Andrade, R. G. (1992). Schema and motivation. In R. G. D'Andrade & C. Strauss (Eds.). *Human motives and cultural models,* New York: Cambridge University Press.

David, D. S., & Brannon, R. (1976). *The forty-nine percent majority: The male sex role.* Reading, MA: Addison-Wesley.

Dobson, J. (1994). *Seven Promises of a Promise Keeper.* Colorado Springs, CO: Focus on the Family.

Grieco, L. (1996). *A qualitative study of Promise Keeper fathers.* Unpublished Psy.D. Research Project, Ferkauf Graduate School of Psychology, Yeshiva University, Bronx, NY.

Harrison, J. (1978). Warning: The male role may be dangerous to your health. *The Journal of Social Issues, 34,* 65–86.

Kerr, M., & Bowen, M. (1988). *Family evaluation.* New York: W. W. Norton. New York: Basic Books.
Kimmel, M. (Ed.). (1997). *Changing men: New directions in research on men and masculinity.* Newbury Park, CA: Sage.
Kimmel, M. (1997). Promise Keepers: Patriarch's second coming as masculine renewal. *Tikkun, 12,* 46–50.
Kimmel, M. (1998). Personal communication.
Kimmel, M., & Kaufman, M. (1995). Weekend warriors: The new men's movement. In M. Kimmel (Ed.), *The politics of manhood: Profeminist men respond to mythopeotic men's movement.* Philadelphia: Temple University Press.
Levant, R. F., & Pollack, W. S. (Eds.). (1995). *A new psychology of men.* New York: Basic Books.
Lewin, T. (1995, May 11). Women are becoming equal providers. *The New York Times,* p. A27.
McCartney, W. (1995). *From ashes to glory.* Nashville, TN: Thomas Nelson Publications.
Messner, M. (1995). Changing men and feminist politics in the U.S. In M. Kimmel (Ed.), *The politics of manhood: Profeminist men respond to the mythopoetic men's movement.* Philadelphia: Temple University Press.
Morgan, D. (1998). *Focus groups as qualitative research.* Newbury Park, CA: Sage.
Patterson, C. J. (1995). Lesbian mothers, gay fathers, and their children. In A. R. D'Augelli & C. J. Patterson (Eds.), *Lesbian, gay, and bisexual identities across the lifespan.* New York: Oxford University Press.
Pleck, J. H. (1993). Are "family supportive" employee policies relevant to men? In J. C. Hood (Ed.), *Men, work, and family.* Newbury Park, CA: Sage.
Pleck, J. H. (1995). The gender role strain paradigm: An update. In R. F. Levant & W. S. Pollack (Eds.), *A new psychology of men.* New York: Basic Books.
Popenoe, D. (1996). *Life without father.* New York: Martin Pressler Press.
Quartironi, B. (1995). *The new gay fathers: An exploratory study of their experiences, perceptions, and concerns.* Unpublished Psy.D. Research Project, Ferkauf Graduate School of Psychology, Yeshiva University, Bronx, NY.
Rich, F. (1996, September 25). Thank God I'm a man. *The New York Times,* p. A21.
Rubin, H. J., & Rubin, I. S. (1995). *Qualitative interviewing: The art of hearing data.* Newbury Park, CA: Sage.
Silverstein, L. B., & Auerbach, C. F. (in press). Deconstructing the essential father. *American Psychologist.*
Strauss, A. L. (1997). *Qualitative analysis for social scientists.* New York: Cambridge University Press.
Strauss, A. L., & Corbin, J. (1997). *Grounded theory in practice.* Thousand Oaks, CA: Sage.
Strauss, A. L., & Corbin, J. (1990). *Basics of qualitative research: Grounded theory procedures and techniques.* Newbury Park, CA: Sage.

Vygotsky, L. S. (1978). *Mind and society.* Cambridge, MA: Harvard University Press.

Weinberg, N. F. (1997). *Fathering experiences of co-providing fathers: A qualitative research study.* Unpublished Psy.D. Research Project, Ferkauf Graduate School of Psychology, Yeshiva University, Bronx, NY.

Wolf, R. (1995, August 8). Men at work: On the power of prayer. *U.S.A. Today,* p. A9.

Silverstein, L. B., Auerbach, C. F., Grieco, L., & Dunkel, F. (1999). Do Promise Keeper fathers dream of feminist sheep? *Sex Roles, 40,* 665–688.

References

Auerbach, C., Silverstein, L., & Zizi, M. (1997). The evolving structure of fatherhood among Haitian Americans. *Journal of African American Men, 2*, 59–85.

Backer-Bolensky, L. (1998). Modern Orthodox Jewish fathers: A qualitative research study. Unpublished Psy.D. Research Project, Ferkauf Graduate School of Psychology, Yeshiva University, Bronx, NY.

Benson, A., Silverstein, L. B., & Auerbach, C. F. (2002). *Can gay fathers contribute to changing cultural norms?* Manuscript in preparation.

Blankenhorn, D. (1995). *Fatherless America: Confronting our most urgent national problem.* New York: Basic Books.

Cath, S. H., Gurwitt, A., & Gunsberg, L. (Eds.). (1989). *Fathers and their families.* Hillsdale, NJ: Analytic Press.

Denzin, N. K., & Lincoln, Y. S. (Eds.). (2000). *Handbook of qualitative research* (2nd. ed.). Thousand Oaks, CA: Sage.

Dunkel, F., Auerbach, C. F., & Silverstein, L. B. (2002). *Stepfathering: Growth through negotiation.* Manuscript in preparation.

Edwards, W. K., & Silverstein, L. B. (2003). *The parenting experiences of young Black fathers: A culturally relevant perspective.* Manuscript in preparation.

Ellis, C., & Bochner, A. P. (2000). Autoethnography, personal narrative, reflexivity: Researcher as subject. In N. K. Denzin & Y. S. Lincoln (Eds.), *Handbook of qualitative research, 2nd. ed.* (pp.733–768). Thousand Oaks, CA: Sage.

Freud, S. (1961). Some psychical consequences to the anatomical distinction between the sexes. In J. Strachey (Ed. & Trans.), *The standard edition of the complete psychological works of Sigmund Freud* (Vol. 19) London: Hogarth Press.

Grieco, L. (1996). A qualitative study of Promise Keeper fathers. Unpublished Psy. D. research project, Ferkauf Graduate School of Psychology, Yeshiva University, Bronx, NY.

Hersch, M., Silverstein, L. B., & Auerbach, C. F. (2003). *"Going somewhere." When early childbearing positively affects a young mother's life.* Manuscript in preparation.

Kohlberg, L. (1981). *The philosophy of moral development.* San Francisco: Harper & Row.

Lamb, M. E. (Ed.) (1987). *The father's role: Cross-cultural perspectives.* Hillsdale, NJ: Erlbaum.

LaRossa, R. (1988). Fatherhood and social change. *Family Relations 37*, 452–457.

LaRossa, R. (1997). *The modernization of fatherhood: A social and political theory.* Chicago: University of Chicago Press.

Mishler, E. G., & Steinitz, V. (2001, January). *Solidarity work: Researchers in the struggle for social justice.* Paper presented at the 14th Annual QUIG Conference on Interdisciplinary Qualitative Studies, Georgia Center for Continuing Education, University of Georgia, Athens.

Oldenburg, C. Z., Silverstein, L. B., Auerbach, C. F., & Peguero, A. (2003). *Creolization. Latino fathers redefining the fathering role.* Manuscript in preparation.

Paragon, M. (1998). Modern Orthodox Jewish Men: A qualitative research project on fatherhood. Unpublished Psy.D. Research Project, Ferkauf Graduate School of Psychology, Yeshiva University, Bronx, NY.

Peguero, A., Silverstein, L. B., & Auerbach, C. F. (1999, August). Effects of immigration on the fathering identities of Dominican men. In R. F. Levant, Chair, *New research on masculinities in ethnocultural perspective.* Symposium presented at the Annual Convention of the American Psychological Association, Boston.

Peguero, A. R., Silverstein, L, B. & Auerbach, C. F. (2000, Winter). Effects of immigration on the fathering identities of Dominican men. *The Family Psychologist Vol. 000,* 12–13.

Pleck, J. H. (1981). *The myth of masculinity.* Cambridge, MA: MIT Press.

Pleck, J. H. (1995). The gender role strain paradigm: An update. In R. F. Levant & W. S. Pollack (Eds.), *A new psychology of men* (pp. 11–32). New York: Basic Books.

Rubin, H. J., & Rubin, I. S. (1995). *Qualitative interviewing: The art of hearing data.* Thousand Oaks, CA: Sage.

Schacher, S., Auerbach, C. F., & Silverstein, L. B. (2003). *Gay fathers redefining fathering and family.* Manuscript in preparation.

Silverman, D. (1993). *Interpreting qualitative data: Methods for analyzing talk, text, and interaction.* Thousand Oaks, CA: Sage.

Silverstein, L. B. (2001). Fathers and families. In J. P. McHale & W. A. Grolnick (Eds.), *Retrospect and prospect in the psychological study of families* (pp. 35–64). Mahwah, NJ: Erlbaum.

Silverstein, L. B. & Auerbach, C. F. (in press). Post-modern families. In J. P. Roopnarine (Ed.) Families in Global Perspective.

Silverstein, L. B., & Auerbach, C. F., Grieco, L., & Dunkel, F. (1999). Do Promise Keeper fathers dream of feminist sheep? *Sex Roles, 40,* 665–688.

Silverstein, L. B., Auerbach, C. F., & Levant, R. (2002). Contemporary fathers reconstructing masculinity: Clinical implications of gender role strain. *Professional Psychology: Research and Practice, 4,* 361–369.

Smith, J. K., & Deemer, D. K. (2000). The problem of criteria in an age of relativism. In N. K. Denzin & Y. S. Lincoln (Eds.), *Handbook of qualitative research, 2nd. ed.* (pp.877–896). Thousand Oaks, CA: Sage.

Snarey, J. (1993). *How fathers care for the next generation. A four decade study.* Cambridge, MA: Harvard University Press.

Solash, D., & Silverstein, L. B. (2000, August). Early childbearing: A resiliency perspective. In G. Bacigalupe & L. B. Silverstein (Co-Chairs), *Silenced voices: Families whose stories have not been heard.* Symposium presented at the annual convention of the American Psychological Association, Washington, DC.

Sue, D. W., & Sue, D. (1990). *Counseling the culturally different. Theory and practice.* New York: Wiley.

Weil, F. (1997). Divorced fathers: A qualitative research study. Unpublished Psy.D. Research Project, Ferkauf Graduate School of Psychology, Yeshiva University, Bronx, NY.

Weinberg, N. (1997). Fathering within the co-providing context. Unpublished Psy.D. Research Project, Ferkauf Graduate School of Psychology, Yeshiva University, Bronx, NY.

Yoder, J. D., & Berendsen, L. L. (2001). "Outsider within" the firehouse: African American and White women firefighters. *Psychology of Women Quarterly, 25,* 27–36.

Zizi, M. J. (1996). A qualitative study of Haitian Christian men's experience as fathers. Unpublished Psy.D. research project, Ferkauf Graduate School of Psychology, Yeshiva University, Bronx, NY.

Index

About the Authors

CARL F. AUERBACH and LOUISE B. SILVERSTEIN are associate professors of psychology at the Ferkauf Graduate School of Psychology at Yeshiva University. They co-direct the Yeshiva Fatherhood Project. Both have published extensively in scholarly journals. Louise B. Silverstein is a former president of the American Psychological Association's Division of Family Psychology.